T0401659

TARANTA

BY JOSÉ DUARTE & ALISON ARNETT

TARANTA

FROM BOSTON TO PERU: A CHEF'S JOURNEY TO SUSTAINABILITY

HISTRIA
PERSPECTIVES

Histria Perspectives
Las Vegas ♦ Chicago ♦ Palm Beach

Published in the United States of America by
Histria Books
7181 N. Hualapai Way, Ste. 130-86
Las Vegas, NV 89166 U.S.A.
HistriaBooks.com

Histria Perspectives is an imprint of Histria Books dedicated to outstanding non-fiction books.

Titles published under the imprints of Histria Books are distributed worldwide.

Library of Congress Control Number: 2024931090

ISBN 978-1-59211-454-2 (casebound)
ISBN 978-1-59211-488-7 (eBook)

Table of CON TEN TS

Photographs by Daniela Talavera

TARANTA

FROM BOSTON TO PERU: A CHEF'S JOURNEY TO SUSTAINABILITY

By Jose Duarte with Alison Arnett

In early August 2020 I posted on social media that Taranta, my restaurant in the North End of Boston, was closing. In the midst of the covid-19 pandemic, mine was one of many closures, but though economic in cause, this marked the end of a chapter.

"Taranta turned 20 years old last month," I wrote. "My wife and I opened this business as a wedding present to each other, and to us, it is our first child. We have been a part of an amazing community, creating memorable experiences and sharing our sustainability efforts."

The last meal at Taranta in the North End was served by the end of that August and the restaurant was shuttered. But the dream did not die.

Chefs write cookbooks all the time – to promote a restaurant, to support a television presence, as testimonials to their talent or as memoirs of childhood. My inspiration is a little different. From childhood, food and cooking have been my obsession, and although I love to give others joy through delicious food, I've always felt that the connections that one makes through food, and through cooking, sharing, talking about it, are my lodestones.

We stand at a crucial point – a time when the fate of the universe is literally in our hands. Sustaining this earth and its peoples is the challenge

A CHEF'S JOURNEY

before us. I think food can show the way. Taranta, my restaurant marrying Peruvian ingredients ingredients with Southern Italian techniques, was a platform for exploring solutions -- from how to delight my patrons to fostering sustainability to discovering ways to enrich the lives of rural Peruvians to supporting and enriching the lives of my employees.

An integral element of my life as a restaurateur is the sustainability of our planet. Although it's a word sometimes tossed around with abandon, for me, sustainability must be tied to us as humans – how we treat each other and the earth on which we depend, and how we help each other when a pandemic sweeps the world. That might mean conserving water in my cooking, lecturing on sustainable seafood, trying to rid the world of plastics dangerous to sea life as well as to humans, or ensuring that workers in my restaurant and on farms are treated fairly. During the pandemic, it meant assuring that my workers not only were safe, but that they could financially take care of themselves and their families. That was the most regrettable part as I faced closing – not being able to employ people.

I never thought that working at Taranta was just a job for my employees, just a way to earn money. I hope that they can grow in personal development, learning about food, about the world and how to relate that to those who eat in the restaurant.

When my co-writer, Alison Arnett and I, began to work on a book, it slowly morphed from a simple cookbook to something broader and more nuanced.

Food is the center of my life, but its impact is felt in many ways and touches many arenas. Yes, Taranta, the North End time-honored establishment, may be gone, but what it stands for endures.

The story of Taranta begins simply with childhood forays to markets in Lima with a native Campa woman who lived with my grandmother. Rosa would go every morning to buy what was needed for the day, and I would tag along. The sights, the aromas, the tastes were intoxicating, and those I met gave me fresh insights. The lady who sold fish let me taste seaweed that had the flavor of the

sea. I learned about the many varieties of potatoes, the jungle fruit first used to cure fish for ceviche, the dizzying array of peppers that subtly spice Peruvian food. My teachers were these market vendors who knew where their food came from and how it could enhance life. For me, the hunger to learn and taste more was ignited and has only strengthened throughout my life.

When my wife and I opened Taranta, it was going to be a Southern Italian restaurant with the bold, earthy flavors of Campania. But in Boston's North End, there were as many as 50 restaurants in about one square mile, and they were mostly Italian. As I tried to establish my Italian restaurant, I found I kept returning to the flavors and ingredients I had left behind, dreaming of how a rocoto pepper from Peru would heat up an Italian sauce or how perfectly lucuma, Peruvian egg fruit, would flavor a tiramisu.

Business was slow at first, so my team and I started experimenting — using quinoa for a risotto, or aji amarillo peppers in a tomato sauce, or making a pesto with huacatay, a Peruvian mint. This marriage of Peru and Italy was noticed, and customers loved the dishes. After a wild period of experimentation, I began to settle down, thinking about why a dish worked, and when it did not. Both Peruvians and Italians view eating as a cultural and social exchange, and they all are passionate about food. Peru, with its many climate zones, from tropical seacoast and jungles to the dry, high altitudes of the Andes, has unique ingredients. And the marriage of the Italian technique and those ingredients works surprisingly well. Like all successful marriages, there's a little mystery involved.

Exploring this mystery — and curiosity about the world —- is what inspires me. Taranta will live again, of that I am sure. As a chef, a restaurateur, a traveler, an environmentalist, I'm always curious – about people, about foods and where they come from, about better ways to live. That is what propels me – a restlessness to see more, to find out how people work and live, to discover ways to make their lives more delicious. In this curiosity, I have found my purpose — to discover how food can help us all sustain our planet and each other in the years ahead.

CHAPTER 1
MY PERU

For me, this is home: anticuchos grilling over open flame; lucuma fruits hanging heavy from trees; the briny snap of ceviche with its sea salt flavors fresh and vivid; a dizzying array of potatoes all just right for a special dish; long lunches with family. These images are only a small glimpse of Peru, its bounty from the sea to the Andes to the lowlands in between.

I spent years of my childhood in Venezuela where my father was working, but I treasured vacations when we would return home to Peru. Going home was like aroma therapy, opening your senses to the smells, tastes and sights of a land where food is of paramount importance.

For a Peruvian, each day is an adventure in eating: Ceviche, even in the morning to cure a hangover. Fruit juices at the city markets where each stand specializes in a particular fruit or bountiful seafood and meat soups. "El Lonche", a Peruvian afternoon institution around tea time with little sandwiches, café con leche, and a little sweet. Pollo a brasa (chargrilled chicken) or chifa (Chinese inspired rice dishes) at dinner time, and maybe a super late-night pork sandwich after a night of dancing. All washed down with Pisco Sours, the national drink of Peru, and cerveza (beer).

These recipes explore the traditional Peru – ceviche made in minutes by the seaside; anticuchos grilled at every roadside stand; causa molded from Peruvian potatoes; chicken roasted over open flames; a whisper of a dessert with the essence of Peruvian limes; roasted pork sandwiches to eat with Pisco Sours. As in Peru, your senses will be awakened.

Recipes:
- » Pollo a la Brasa
- » Lobster Causa
- » Beef Heart Anticucho
- » Peruvian Pork Sandwiches
- » Sancochado
- » Pulpo al Olivo
- » Suspiro Limeno
- » Classic Pisco Sour

POLLO A LA BRASA

The spice rub on this delicious grilled chicken makes for a perfect summer dish. Since the sauce can be made ahead and the chicken marinated overnight, it's easy to have ready for a dinner party. This recipe is a simplified version of the traditional pollo a la brasa that is normally cooked on a charcoal rotisserie.

16

SERVES 4

INGREDIENTS

For the Marinade
- » 1 whole chicken, 2 ½-3 pound (broiler size) cut into 8 pieces
- » 4 teaspoons kosher salt
- » 1 cup light beer
- » ⅓ cup soy sauce
- » ½ cup of mild panca pepper paste
- » 2 tablespoons ground cumin
- » 1 tablespoon paprika
- » 1/2 teaspoon freshly ground black pepper
- » ½ cup of Peruvian garlic paste
- » ½ cup white vinegar
- » 4 tablespoons vegetable or canola oil
- » 2 tablespoons huacatay (Peruvian black mint) paste
- » 1 tablespoon aji amarillo paste

For the Sauce:
- » 2 tablespoons aji amarillo pepper paste
- » 2 teaspoons honey
- » ½ teaspoon Dijon mustard
- » 1 cup mayonnaise
- » 1 ½ cup fresh cilantro leaves
- » 2 medium garlic cloves
- » 2 jalapenos, ribs and seeds removed
- » 2 teaspoons vegetable oil
- » 4 tablespoons fresh squeezed lime juice
- » Kosher salt and freshly ground black pepper
- » 1 tablespoon huacatay paste

DIRECTIONS:

1. In a medium-sized bowl, whisk together the marinade ingredients. Place the 8 chicken pieces in a rectangular glass baking dish, large enough to also hold the marinade. Pour the marinade over the chicken, and turn the pieces to cover both sides. Marinate at least six hours and up to 24 hours.

2. For the sauce, combine the sauce ingredients in a blender jar or in a food processor, and blend at high speed, scraping down the sides as needed. The result should be a smooth creamy mixture; season with salt and pepper. Transfer the mixture to a squirt bottle or container and store it in the refrigerator.

3. Preheat the grill to 500 degrees; if your grill has a cover keep it closed. Then open the cover, and using half an onion dipped lightly in vegetable oil, rub the onion over the grill to clean it.

4. Place chicken on the grill, skin side down and sear for about 5 minutes until grill marks appear on the skin, then flip it over so the skin side is facing up. Lower the grill temperature to medium and cook, while periodically brushing it with some of the marinade. Cover the grill and cook for about 8 minutes more. Cooking time can vary so it is recommendable to use a meat thermometer; the internal temperature should reach 165°F.

5. Serve with the sauce on the side.

17

LOBSTER CAUSA

Causa, a traditional Peruvian potato dish, was created during the War of the Pacific, in which Peru and Bolivia fought against Chile. The dish came to symbolize the efforts of the women to gather food for the causa (cause) of the soldiers. Generally served chilled as a great summer dish, it can also be made with crab, smoked trout, or other fish.

SERVES 4

INGREDIENTS

- » 2 pounds yellow Peruvian potatoes, halved or quartered
- » 4 tablespoons aji amarillo paste
- » 1/4 cup vegetable oil
- » Juice of 1 key lime
- » 1/2 pound lobster meat
- » 3/4 cup mayonnaise
- » 1/2 onion, finely chopped
- » 1/2 shallot, finely chopped
- » ½ stalk celery, finely chopped (optional)
- » 1 ripe avocado
- » 1 ripe tomato
- » Salt and pepper
- » 6 Peruvian Botija olives

LOBSTER CAUSA

DIRECTIONS:

1. Steam the potatoes for about 10-15 minutes until easily pierced by a fork. Mash while still warm with a potato ricer, adding ½ teaspoon salt and ½ teaspoon pepper.

2. Let cool and then mix thoroughly with the aji amarillo paste, vegetable oil, lime juice, and more salt to taste.

3. Saving about ¼ cup lobster meat, mix the rest with half the mayonnaise, chopped onions and shallots, celery if desired, and some lime juice. Season to taste.

4. Place a layer of mashed potatoes on a serving dish, and spread with a thin film of mayonnaise. Cover with lobster salad. Chop the avocado and tomato and lay on top of the lobster salad.

5. Cover with another layer of potatoes, and top with Botija olives and the rest of the lobster meat.

BEEF HEART ANTICUCHO

These skewers are very popular street food in Peru where the aroma from grilling meat fills the air and eager customers line up at their favorite stands. Veal heart can be substituted. For those not fond of organ meats, hanger steak or even beef tenderloin can be used.on a charcoal rotisserie.

SERVES 4

INGREDIENTS

- » 1 pound beef heart, trimmed of silverskin and fat
- » 1 tablespoon Peruvian garlic paste
- » 3-4 tablespoons aji panca paste
- » ½ cup sherry vinegar
- » 1 tablespoon ground cumin
- » 2 teaspoons dried oregano
- » ½ tablespoon paprika
- » ½ cup canola oil
- » Salt, pepper to taste

DIRECTIONS:

1. Cut the beef heart or other meat into 1 ½-inch chunks and place in a large bowl.

2. For the marinade, place all ingredients except the meat in a blender, and mix until well combined.

3. Pour marinade over beef heart or meat chunks and refrigerate for at least 2 hours or overnight.

4. Place beef heart or meat chunks on metal or heat-proof skewers, making sure not to pack them too closely together to allow even cooking on all sides. Grill them over a medium-high fire for 2 to 3 minutes on each side, generously brushing them with the marinade during the grilling process.

PERUVIAN PORK SANDWICHES
(PAN CON CHICHARRÓN)

Peruvian pan con chicharrón is a specially prepared sandwich where the main ingredient is pork fried in its own fat. Chicharrón, regardless of its main ingredient, is a true delight. In Peru, it takes center stage during breakfast.

SERVES 4

INGREDIENTS

» 1 pound fresh pork belly, skin on
» Coarse sea salt
» 1 large sweet potato
» Salt
» ½ cup of vegetable oil
» 1 large red onion
» ½ cup mint leaves, chopped
» Juice of 2 limes
» 1 tablespoon white vinegar
» 4 Banh Mi rolls (Vietnamese Baguette)

DIRECTIONS:

To roast the belly

1. Place the pork belly skin side up and score the skin 1-inch apart with the tip of a razor blade or utility knife. This will help remove excess water for a crispy texture.

2. Season the top of the belly with coarse sea salt; cover with plastic wrap and refrigerate overnight.

3. The next day, remove any excess liquid by drying the skin with a paper towel. Place the belly in a deep roasting pan. Preheat the oven to 250 degrees F.

4. Place the pan in the oven and slow roast for 2 ¼ hours. Then increase the temperature to 450F for about 5 minutes until the skin becomes crispy, achieving the crackling "chicharrón" effect. If the skin does not get crispy, put under the oven broil to crisp; watch carefully so that it doesn't burn.

5. Remove from oven and let it cool for a few minutes

To make the fried sweet potatoes

1. Peel the sweet potatoes, and cut into about 1-inch thick lengthwise pieces.

2. Put ½ cup of vegetable oil in a large frying pan and add the sweet potato slices, turning until golden brown and tender. Remove with a slotted spoon onto a plate lined with paper towels to drain oil.

To make the Salsa Criolla topping

1. Slice the onion very thin and place into a bowl. Add the chopped mint, lime juice and vinegar. Mix lightly.

To assemble the sandwiches

1. Place the cooked pork belly on a cutting board, crispy skin side up. Using a serrated bread knife, cut into 1-inch slices.

2. Lightly toast the Banh Mi roll. Cut the rolls in half and place the fried sweet potatoes on the bottom, then the pork belly and then the criolla salad. Place the top of the roll on and press lightly to keep the ingredients in the roll. Repeat with the remaining three rolls.

SANCOCHADO

This hearty dish from northern Peru is a favorite of my maternal grandmother. It is similar to the French pot au feu or Italian bollito misto. The broth is a healthy side benefit, akin to bone broth.

SERVES 6-8

24

INGREDIENTS

- » 2 ½ lbs beef chuck roast
- » 4 large carrots, sliced into ½ inch rounds
- » 1 celery stalk, sliced
- » 2 large onions, quartered
- » 1-2 teaspoons salt
- » 1-2 teaspoons pepper
- » 2 teaspoons oregano
- » ½ lb peeled yuca root, cut into chunks
- » 2 large potatoes, each divided in 3 pieces
- » 1 cabbage, quartered
- » 2 semi-ripe plantains, each cut into 3 pieces
- » 2 ears fresh corn, each cut into 6 pieces

DIRECTIONS:

1. Put the meat, celery, carrots and onions in a large saucepan or stockpot, and cover with water. Bring to a boil, and skim foam if necessary. Add salt, pepper and oregano, turn the heat to medium low and cover with a lid. Simmer for 2 ½ hours until the meat is fork tender, skimming every now and then.

2. When the meat is tender, add the potatoes and yucca, and cook for about 20 more minutes until these vegetables are also tender. Add cabbage and cook for 15-20 minutes more. Add more salt and pepper to taste.

3. Meanwhile, in a separate saucepan, cover plantains with water and boil until tender, about 20 minutes. In another saucepan, bring water to boil and add corn, cooking for about 10 minutes until tender. Let the plantains and corn cool slightly.

4. Slice the meat on a cutting board and place it in the center of a large platter. Using a slotted spoon, remove the potatoes, yucca and cabbage from the broth and arrange, along with the plantains and corn, around the meat.

5. Strain the cooking broth, serving it separately from a soup tureen. The sancochado can be accompanied with salsa criolla (167 page).

PULPO AL OLIVO

SERVES 3

INGREDIENTS

- » 3 pounds octopus or 4 large cooked tentacles, frozen, if available
- » 2 eggs
- » 1 ½ cup (or a little less) extra virgin olive oil
- » 20 pitted Botija olives
- » 3 tablespoons lime juice

26

DIRECTIONS:

1. In a large pot, place the octopus and cover with water; bring it to boil for about 30 minutes until the octopus is soft. Remove, let it cool down and cut tentacles and freeze, (freezing the cooked octopus will help tenderize it). Remove from the freezer and let it thaw. Slice thinly.

2. To make a simple mayonnaise using an immersion blender, put eggs in a large bowl, and blend for a few seconds to mix. Begin adding olive oil drop by drop, blending constantly until mixture is thick and emulsified. Then add the olives and the lime juice. (You can also substitute with a good brand of commercial mayonnaise, adding the olives at the end.)

3. Place slices of octopus on a flat dish and coat them with the olive mayonnaise sauce.

SUSPIRO LIMENO

This heavenly dessert, inspired by sabayon, is easy to make and very impressive. My grandmother made it often, because the farm hens produced an abundance of eggs.

SERVES 4-6

INGREDIENTS

For the Marinade
- » 12-ounce can evaporated milk
- » 14-ounce can sweetened condensed milk
- » 3 eggs, separated
- » 2 tablespoons liqueur (rum, Pisco, Port wine)
- » 1 cup sugar
- » Pinch of cream of tartar

DIRECTIONS:

1. n a heavy-bottomed saucepan, pour in evaporated milk and sweetened condensed milk. Heat to just under boiling and then simmer until the mixture is a golden caramel color and quite thick. Take off heat; stir egg yolks in a bowl and add to warm milk, stirring until silky.

2. Add liqueur.

3. Heat sugar in a small, heavy-bottomed pan until liquid. Continue at a boil until soft-ball stage (240 degrees on a candy thermometer.)

4. Whip egg whites until soft peaks form. Beat in the caramelized sugar until the mixture is cool.

5. In a cocktail or wine glass, pour the egg/milk mixture into the bottom. Then top with whipped egg whites, teased into peaks.

CLASSIC PISCO SOUR

Variations are endless, but the classic pisco sour is still the standard in Peru. Perfectly refreshing on a hot day, it's also traditional with roast pork sandwiches after a night of clubbing.

SERVES 1

INGREDIENTS

- » 2 ounces Peruvian Pisco, such as Pisco La Caravedo
- » ¾ ounce simple syrup
- » ¾ ounce lime juice
- » 1 egg white
- » Crushed ice
- » 2 to 3 dashes Angostura bitters

DIRECTIONS:

In a cocktail shaker, mix pisco, simple syrup, lime juice and egg white ice and shake vigorously for at least 30 seconds, proceed to strain into a coupe or cocktail glass. Add 3 dashes of Angostura Bitters.

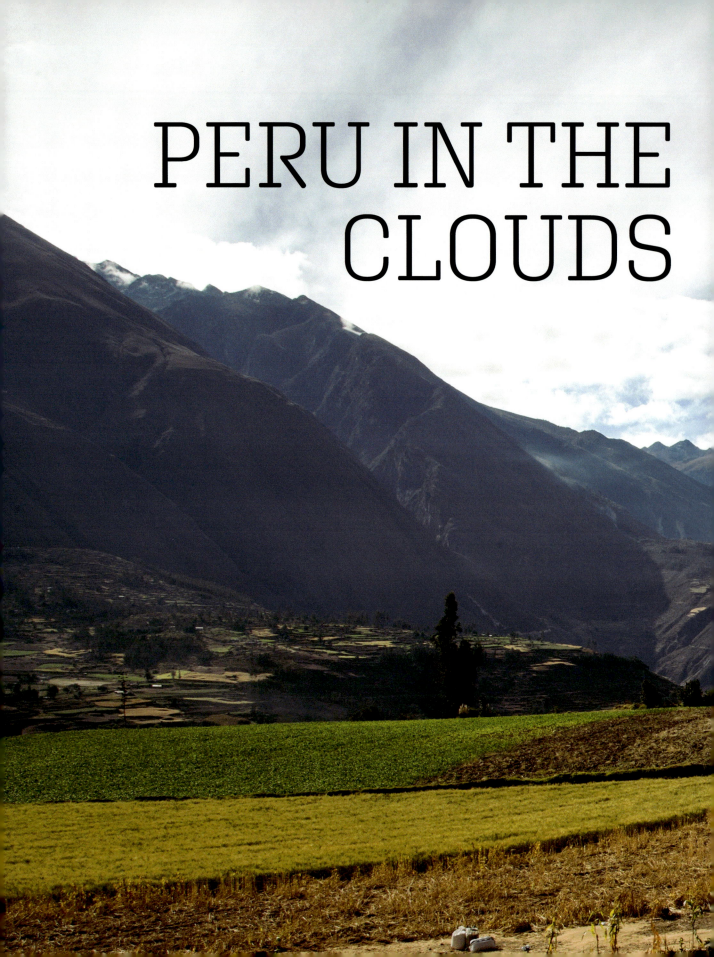

PERU IN THE CLOUDS

GRANDMA PAULINA AND THE POWER OF SUPERFOODS

My grandmother on my father's side, Paulina, grew up in the jungle near La Merced. Her father, Antonio Mungi, was an Italian immigrant who built a farm from stone that he called Hacienda Roma. The farm produced sugar cane that my great-grandfather used in his distillery to make aguardiente; the distillery is still in operation.

My grandmother's knowledge of medicinal plants was very extensive, and she brought her deep belief in the healing powers of native plants when she moved to Lima with my grandfather. When I was a child, she would give me oregano for stomach cramps, lemon verbena for digestion after dinner, and dried tara for sore throats. In her garden were caigua plants with fruit that looked like long gourds. She said that this native plant was used by the Incas, and could lower blood pressure.

In the city, she went to the sprawling food markets to find sacha inchi oil, pressed from the nut of an Amazonian plant that is also called the Inca peanut. This oil is very high in protein and rich in omega 3, double that of olive oil. This she used for salads. Or she would buy chuño (freeze-dried) potatoes to make a paste, something like a gelatin, with orange and sugar to treat upset stomachs.

For Peruvians, using natural ingredients to sustain or promote health is ingrained in our food culture. At a "farmacia" at a local market in the Amazon Basin, there are herbs to help lower blood pressure, to ease depression, and to improve kidney function. At one market, a vendor told me, smiling, that a certain tree mold would help a stingy person open his wallet.

Many of the so-called superfoods originated in Peru. Some of these, such as amaranth (also called kiwicha), camu camu berries, maca root, tarwi (lupini beans), tocosh (fermented potatoes), or even more common foods such as cacao or quinoa, would have been familiar to my grandmother, and are still used in Peru. Throughout this book, you will find references and recipes that share Peruvian knowledge on improving your health through natural ingredients.

33

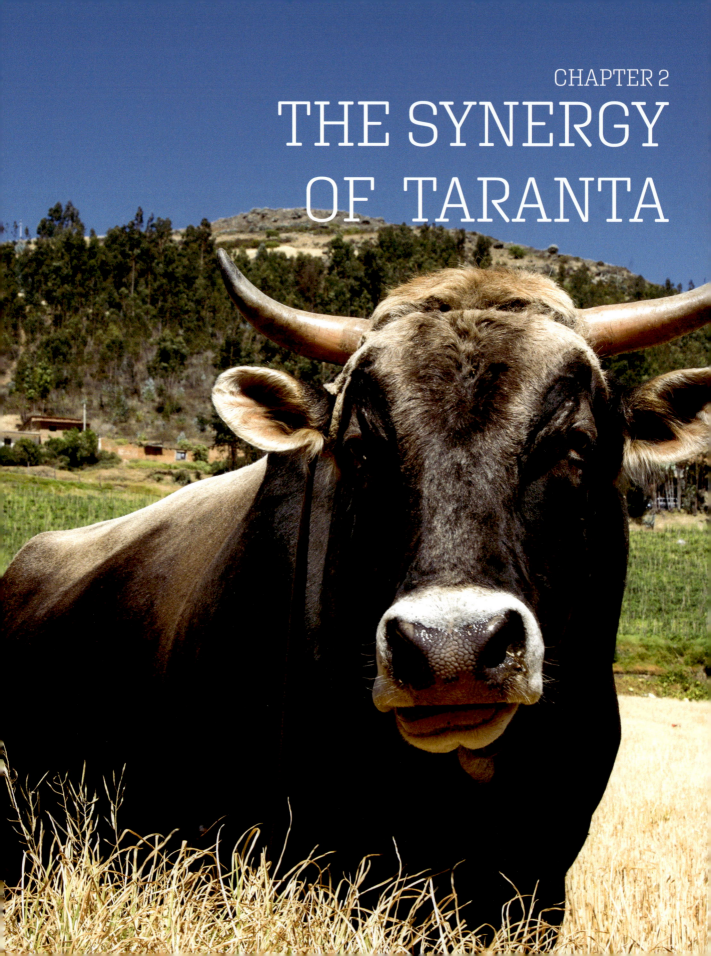

CHAPTER 2

THE SYNERGY OF TARANTA

Taranta, the restaurant, started as a tribute to Southern Italy with authentic dishes from Campania, Sicily, and Calabria. But spurred by homesickness for Peru and curiosity, my cooks and I started improvising. Could yucca stand in for potatoes in a gnocchi recipe? Could the luscious Peruvian fruit lucuma enrich a semifreddo?

My imagination expanded the horizons with every experiment, and soon customers were clamoring for our fusion of Peruvian ingredients with Italian sensibility. Over many years, we drew customers with our cross-cultural dishes, and at the same time imparted knowledge about the fruits and vegetables, fish, and spices of a country far away.

Taranta was not just an island of cuisine. My commitment to bettering the environment for my children and others drove a campaign to make the restaurant as "green" as possible. From reusing cooking oil to run the sporty Taranta truck to installing low flush toilets to composting to offering only biodynamic wines, my staff and I worked to integrate the principle of saving the earth along with feeding our customers. Along with those goals which continue in my other restaurants, Tambo 22 and Trattoria San Pietro, I have always searched for sustainable food sources: Organic eggs from a local farm; seafood sourced from a local company that works directly with New England fishermen and women; wine sourced from small, dedicated distributors specializing in organic and biodynamic wines; pastries, beers and even nuts seasoned with Peruvian flavors from small, dedicated creators.

Recipes:
- » Grilled Trout with Pallares
- » Peruvian-Style Lamb Ragu with Yucca Gnocchi
- » Espresso Crusted Beef Tenderloin
- » Spaghetti with Sea Urchin
- » Lucuma Semifreddo

35

All of this is reflected on the plate and communicated to our customers, giving them an experience that extends far beyond merely picking up a menu at the beginning and plunking down a credit card at the end. But none of this would have been possible at Taranta without staff members who believed in what the restaurant stood for. In an industry where turnover and instability are taken for granted, Taranta's cooks, servers and hosts stayed for years. Many restaurateurs talk about their restaurant families, but Taranta's employees looked out for each other and for the restaurant to an astonishing degree. From Ricardo, a very talented cook from rural El Salvador who was taught to read and write by coworkers while he was a dishwasher at Taranta, to our manager Taylor, who passed up a more lucrative corporate restaurant job because she knew she would learn more and be valued at Taranta, the loyal staff made the restaurant hum, and their energy enhanced the customers' experiences. And the yearly staff trips to Peru or southern Italy, which I designed to educate and broaden the staff members' cuisine and wine knowledge, gave them incentive to work even harder.

Although sadly, Taranta closed after a remarkable 20 years in business on Hanover Street in the North End during the pandemic, my position as a chef, teacher, and speaker is well established in Boston and beyond, and I'm looking forward to my next adventures. The creative force to experiment linking two cuisines joined by a love of food never ends. Taranta lives on.

GRILLED TROUT
WITH PALLARES AND SAFFRON BUTTER

When I visited my wife's ancestral village in Southern Italy, I ate a humble dish of polenta topped with wild greens, beans and potatoes, called "Pizza e Mallone". I began to think of ways to use Peruvian ingredients to recreate the earthiness of this dish. And then I embellished those elements with the sophistication of saffron butter to make a simple but fascinating dish suitable for a dinner party. Oval terracotta dishes like the ones from Peru's Central Highlands conduct heat beautifully and make for a stunning presentation.

SERVES 6

INGREDIENTS

- » 2 cups giant Peruvian lima beans or pallares, soaked overnight (or substitute cannellini beans)
- » 3 tablespoons extra virgin olive oil, divided
- » 3 tablespoons garlic, chopped, divided
- » 1 celery stalk, chopped
- » 1 small carrot, peeled and chopped
- » 1 small onion, chopped
- » 1 bay leaf
- » 3 cups vegetable or chicken stock
- » Salt, pepper to taste
- » ½ cup (I stick) unsalted butter, at room temperature
- » ¼ teaspoon saffron threads
- » 6 8-ounce boned rainbow trout
- » 6 whole yellow Peruvian potatoes or substitute Yukon gold potatoes, steamed and peeled
- » 1 head of escarole, cut into 3-inch lengths

GRILLED TROUT

DIRECTIONS:

1. First prepare the pallares: Heat a large heavy pot over medium heat, add 2 tablespoons olive oil and 1 tablespoon chopped garlic, celery, carrots and onions until onions and garlic are golden (do not allow to burn). Add the drained pallares, broth, and bay leaf, and cook over medium heat for 30 minutes until the beans are just tender. Add salt and pepper and cook for 10-15 minutes more.

2. To make saffron butter: Whisk butter and saffron in a small saucepan over low heat to extract the saffron flavor without browning the butter. Season to taste with sea salt and pepper. Remove from heat.

3. Escarole and setting up plates: Heat a large sauté pan, add 2 tablespoons olive oil and 2 tablespoons garlic, sauté for 2 minutes. Add escarole and sauté for 1 minute more, just until escarole is slightly wilted. Divide escarole and pallares among 6 11-inch oval terracotta dishes, and place one potato on the bottom of each dish.

4. Trout preparation: Preheat grill to medium-high or heat grill pan on top of stove over medium high heat. Season fish with salt and pepper, inside and out. Coat each fish with ½ tablespoon olive oil. Grill the fish until the skin is golden and crispy, 4-5 minutes each side.

5. Preheat the oven to 350 degrees. Place grilled trout on top of pallares mixture. Place 1 teaspoon of saffron butter inside each fish, and brush the fish with saffron butter. Place in the oven for 10 or 12 minutes. Remove terracotta dishes from the oven and brush the trout again with saffron butter and squeeze lemon juice over them.

6. Serve immediately. Fish, beans and vegetables can be served in terracotta dishes (place on heat-resistant tablemats) or on plates.

PERUVIAN STYLE LAMB RAGU
WITH YUCCA GNOCCHI

In Peru and other South American countries, yucca is often eaten with a dry beef ragu or goat ragu. One day I was eating this ragu and realized that yucca would be a perfect crossover for Italian gnocchi. We mixed yucca with potato, and after trial and error, got the right consistency for the gnocchi. And, though an early version was made with goat, Taranta's ragu is made with lamb. In the style of northern Peru, the lamb is marinated in beer or chicha de jora (fermented corn cider) and seasoned with lots of spices and cilantro. The dish is so popular that it was on Taranta's menu for over a decade.

SERVES 6

FOR LAMB RAGU INGREDIENTS

- » 1 ¾ pounds lamb (shoulder or leg)
- » ½ cup white wine vinegar
- » 1 teaspoon cumin
- » 3 cloves garlic, minced
- » ½ cup cilantro, roughly chopped
- » ¼ cup olive oil
- » ½ teaspoon salt
- » ½ teaspoon black pepper
- » 8 ounces beer or Chicha de Jora (corn liquor)
- » 3-4 tablespoons olive oil
- » 1 large red onion, minced
- » 4 teaspoons aji amarillo paste
- » 1 teaspoon rocoto pepper paste
- » 1-2 cups chicken or beef stock

LAMB RAGU WITH YUCCA GNOCCHI

FOR LAMB RAGU DIRECTIONS:

1. Cut the meat into approximately 2-inch cubes. In a blender or food processor, mix the vinegar, cumin, garlic, cilantro, 1/4 cup olive oil, salt and pepper, and pour over the meat in a bowl or deep pan. Pour beer over the top. Let meat marinate in the refrigerator overnight.

2. The next day, heat 3-4 tablespoons of oil in a large pot or skillet on high heat. Working in 2 batches, remove the meat from the marinade, and over medium high heat, brown it on all sides. Remove meat to a plate.

3. Lower the heat, and add the onion and aji amarillo and rocoto pepper pastes to the same skillet. Saute until brown. Then add the meat and the leftover marinade. Add chicken stock and more beer or chicha de jora to cover the meat. Cover and cook for at least 1 1/2 hours until the lamb is very tender.

FOR YUCCA GNOCCHI INGREDIENTS

- » 2 pounds frozen peeled yucca, thawed
- » 1 tablespoon canola oil
- » 1 pound russet potatoes
- » 1 ½ cups all-purpose flour
- » 3 tablespoons grated Parmesan Reggiano, divided
- » 1 egg, beaten lightly
- » Handful of cilantro leaves
- » Salt and pepper

FOR YUCCA GNOCCHI DIRECTIONS:

1. Preheat the oven to 400. Cut yucca into several pieces. Place on a baking sheet, drizzle with oil, and turn to coat. Roast for 30-35 minutes until tender. Meanwhile, peel and cut potatoes into chunks, place in a saucepan of cold water, bring to boil and cook for 10-12 minutes until tender.

2. While the potatoes and yucca are still hot, press both through a potato ricer and then let the mixtures cool. Once cooled, combine them with the egg and the flour; season with salt and pepper, and add 1 tablespoon Parmesan; mix to form a dough. Knead gently (do not apply too much strength because yucca can develop heavy gluey starch).

3. Form the dough into a long rope like a snake and cut into pieces, about ½ inch, with a knife so the sections look like little pillows.

4. Cook gnocchi in salted boiling water for 3 to 5 minutes until they float. Mix the cooked gnocchi with the warm sauce; garnish with the remainder of Parmesan and a few cilantro leaves.

MINI
CALZONCINI
FRITTI

MINI CALZONCINI FRITTI

3 dozen little calzoncini

Italians love their calzones, little packages of soft dough wrapped around a savory filling, similar to Latin America empanadas. Here are three different fillings with distinctly Peruvian flavors -- one with meat and egg, one with mozzarella and a Peruvian olive called botija, and one with bacalao or salt cod. At the restaurant, we serve a variety for appetizers. These calzoncinis would also be wonderful for a dinner party or a buffet.

INGREDIENTS

- » 1 cup water
- » ¾ cup lard
- » 2 3/4 cups flour
- » 2 teaspoons sea salvt

DIRECTIONS:

1. Heat water and lard in a 1-quart saucepan over medium heat until the lard melts, about 3 minutes; let cool slightly.

2. Whisk flour and salt in a large bowl; make a well in the center of the flour mixture. Slowly stir in a lard mixture until a wet dough forms.

3. Using your hands, knead until the dough is smooth, about 2 minutes. Split the dough into two balls; flatten each slightly into discs. Wrap each in plastic wrap; chill for 2 hours. Dough can be refrigerated for up to two days.

* Good quality empanada wrappers can be substituted

MEAT CALZONCINI

Makes 1 dozen calzoncini

INGREDIENTS

- » 2 tablespoon extra virgin olive oil
- » 1 large white onion, finely chopped
- » 1 pound beef tenderloin or sirloin, cut into small dice
- » ¼ teaspoon ground cumin
- » 1 teaspoon Peruvian garlic paste or 1 large garlic clove, mashed in a press
- » 1 tablespoon golden raisins
- » 2 hard boiled egg, chopped

DIRECTIONS:

1. Heat oil in a 12-inch skillet over medium-high heat. Add olive oil and onion and cook until soft.

2. Season beef with salt, add to pan, add cumin and garlic, and cook until browned, add golden raisins and continue cooking for 15 minutes, then transfer mix to a bowl; set aside.

3. Add diced hard-boiled eggs and stir; let cool. Taste for salt.

BACALAO

Makes 1 dozen calzoncini

INGREDIENTS

- » 1 pound salt cod
- » 1 tablespoon extra virgin olive oil
- » ½ white onion, diced fine
- » 1 carrot, diced fine
- » 2 celery stalks, diced fine
- » 1 tablespoon Peruvian garlic paste
- » 1 teaspoon dried oregano
- » 1 can Italian cherry tomatoes
- » ½ cup breadcrumbs

DIRECTIONS:

1. Soak the cod 24 hours or more to remove salt, changing the water at least 2 or 3 times. Cut cod into small pieces. In a medium size saucepan over medium to high heat, sauté onion, carrots and celery with the Peruvian garlic until vegetables are light brown.Then add the cod pieces and cook for about 5 minutes.

2. Add oregano and Italian cherry tomatoes, and juice from the can, and cook for about 15 minutes. Adjust consistency with breadcrumbs to result in a thick mixture. Set aside and let it cool.

MOZZARELLA, LEEKS AND botija OLIVES

Makes 1 dozen calzoncini

INGREDIENTS

- » 1 tablespoon extra virgin olive oil
- » 1 leek, chopped
- » ½ cup heavy cream
- » 3/4 pound fresh mozzarella cheese, chopped
- » 12 botija olives, pits removed
- » Salt, pepper to taste

DIRECTIONS:

1. In a small saucepan over medium heat sauté the chopped leeks with olive oil until they are soft. Add heavy cream and cook slowly until leeks are fully cooked, add salt, set aside to cool.

2. In a medium size bowl, mix mozzarella with braised leeks. Each calzoncini will need a botija olive, added individually.

SHAPING THE CALZONCINIS:

1. For the meat calzoncinis: Roll the dough as thin as possible and cut out a round disc shape, using biscuit cutters or cookie cutters, about 3 ½ inches in diameter. Alternatively, pinch off small balls of dough and roll out one by one.

2. Place a teaspoonful of filling in the middle of each disc. The amount of filling will vary based on the size of the calzoncini, but in general, it's easier to seal one that isn't overstuffed. Also, the more you make them, the easier it becomes to stuff them to the max and still seal them properly.

3. To seal the calzoncinis, fold the disc in half and seal the edges by pressing the dough with your fingers. If you're having difficulty sealing the edges, brush the inside edges with egg white-- it will act as a glue. Then twist and knot edges all around (see illustration)

4. For bacalao calzoncinis: Roll out and cut as above. Place a teaspoonful of the bacalao mixture in the center of each disc. To seal, fold the disc in half and seal the edges by pressing the dough with your fingers, then press with a fork, leaving the fork marks.

5. For mozzarella and olive calzoncinis: Roll and cut as above. Place cheese-leek mixture by spoonfuls on disc and then place a bojita olive on top. Fold the dough in half over the filling. Gently press all the air out. Take the center and squish the filling upwards slightly with your thumb. Press together with your thumb to seal. Fold the back side so it has a round shape as a tortellini.

TO FRY THE CALZONCINI:

INGREDIENTS

» About 1 ½ cups canola oil, enough to go halfway up the sides of the calzoncini ¼ cup cilantro

DIRECTIONS:

1. In a large, deep-sided frying pan, heat oil to 350 degrees, using a meat thermometer to check.

2. Add a layer of calzoncini to cover the bottom of the pan. Do not crowd.

3. Fry until golden on the bottom, then turn and fry the other side. Remove with a slotted spoon or stiff spatula and drain on a platter covered with two layers of paper towels.

4. Reheat the oil to 350 degrees, adding more oil if it is not enough to come halfway up the sides of the calzoncini. Repeat the frying for remaining calzoncini.

DIRECTIONS:

1. Preheat the oven to 400 degrees. Put sweet potatoes into a large roasting pan. Toss with 1 tablespoon olive oil, salt and pepper. Cover with aluminum foil and roast until the yams are tender, about 40 minutes. Peel and put into a food processor. Mix at high speed, and then add butter; mix until the mixture is thick and silky. Keep warm.

2. Trim away any fat or silverskin from beef tenderloins. Wash escarole, dry with kitchen towel, and coarsely chop.

3. Thinly slice sweet potatoes. Heat 2 tablespoons vegetable oil, and fry sweet potatoes until crispy; drain on paper towels. This will be used as garnish. Mix carob syrup and vincotto to make a sauce.

4. Coarsely grind espresso beans in a coffee grinder. Season meat and cover with ground espresso, pressing down to adhere espresso to beef. Heat 2 tablespoons vegetable oil in a frying pan. Sear meat on high heat, 2 minutes a side, and place in a 300-degree oven to keep warm.

5. Heat remaining olive oil in a deep-sided saute pan and add chopped garlic, sauteeing 4 minutes until golden. Add chopped escarole, toss with garlic, and saute about 4 minutes more until escarole is wilted.

6. Warm cream slightly in the microwave oven or in a small pan on the stove. Stir warm cream into yam puree; season with salt and pepper. Slice each portion of beef tenderloin thinly onto warmed plates. Place yam puree on the bottom first, then escarole, meat, and sprinkle sweet potato chips on top and drizzle vincotto mix.

SPAGHETTI WITH SEA URCHIN

Marrying the sensibility of Italy to the ingredients of Peru can lead to discoveries. This umami-rich pasta dish will beguile your guests, and it takes minutes to make.

SERVES 4-6

INGREDIENTS

- » 2 tablespoons extra virgin olive oil
- » 1 teaspoon minced garlic
- » 2 anchovy filets
- » 2 teaspoons aji amarillo paste
- » 2 teaspoons capers
- » 14 ounces Spaghetti di Gragnano, long pasta shape of Trafilata al Bronzo, or other artisanal pasta
- » 4 ounces grated Sardinian bottarga di muggine
- » 6 ounces fresh sea urchin (uni)
- » Sea salt and black pepper
- » Chopped parsley

DIRECTIONS:

1. In a large saute pan, add olive oil, minced garlic, aji amarillo paste, and anchovy filets. Saute until garlic is golden brown, about 8 minutes, smashing the anchovy filets against the sides of the pan to dissolve them. Add capers and set aside.

2. Bring a large pot of water, liberally salted, to a boil. Add pasta and cook until al dente, reserving ½ cup pasta water. Drain pasta and add to oil mixture in a saute pan.

3. Then put in sea urchin and mix vigorously, while adding pasta water slowly until the liquid texture is like a carbonara sauce. Season with salt, sparingly because the anchovies and capers will be salty, and pepper to taste. Dish into serving plates, topping each portion with a tablespoon or so of bottarga and a sprinkling of parsley.

LUCUMA SEMIFREDDO
WITH QUINOA BRITTLE AND CHOCOLATE SAUCE

The prized fruit of the coastal highlands is not only seductively and subtly sweet but also high in antioxidants, fiber and vitamins. Lucuma's butterscotch flavor makes it a wonderful base for this semi-frozen custard derived from an Italian classic.

57

SERVES 8

INGREDIENTS

» 1 cup condensed milk
» 1 cup lucuma pulp
» 1 tablespoon lucuma powder
» 1 cup heavy cream

DIRECTIONS:

1. Chill a metal bowl in the freezer. In another medium-sized bowl, preferably with a spout, mix the condensed milk with the lucuma pulp. Refrigerate while you whip the cream.

2. Remove the chilled bowl and whip the cream until soft peaks form. Fold the whipped cream into the condensed milk-lucuma mixture. Sprinkle lucuma powder over the top and fold in.

3. Put 8 small ring molds onto a tray, pour the lucuma mixture into the molds. Alternatively, pour the mixture into small glasses for an unmolded version. Freeze at least 1 hour to 1 ½ hours or up to 12 hours. To unmold the rings, warm by rolling between your hands. The semifreddo should pop out.

QUINOA BRITTLE INGREDIENTS

» ½ cup white quinoa
» Dash of salt
» 3 tablespoons sugar

DIRECTIONS:

1. Preheat the oven to 375 degrees.

2. Put quinoa and salt into a saucepan and cover with water. Bring to a boil, lower to a simmer and cook for about 10 minutes until the quinoa is slightly soft.

3. Drain, shaking to remove moisture, and spread onto a tray. Sprinkle it with sugar, and place the tray into the oven. Roast for 15 minutes, turning several times. Remove, allow to cool and crumble brittle into small pieces.

CAROB AND CHOCOLATE SAUCE INGREDIENTS

» 1 tablespoon carob syrup
» 4 ounces dark chocolate, 60 percent cacao
» 1 tablespoon water
» 1 tablespoon whipping cream

DIRECTIONS:

1. In a small, heavy-bottomed saucepan, melt chocolate with syrup over medium-low heat. Add water and stir; then add cream to make a smooth sauce.

2. To assemble, using a spoon, splatter a little chocolate sauce onto 8 dessert plates. Pop each semifreddo out and center on the plate. Sprinkle brittle on top of the semifreddo and garnish plate with sliced strawberries, kiwi, blueberries or fruit of your choice. If using the unmolded version, dribble a little chocolate sauce over each glass of semifreddo and garnish with shards of quinoa brittle.

58

WHY I PREFER GRASS-FED

Recipes in Taranta specify grass-fed beef. I believe grass fed is better for you because the result is leaner, more flavorful beef with more beneficial omega 3 and other acids. Grass-fed animals also are not fed antibiotics, unlike commercially raised beef cattle that are given to them to counteract digestive problems from eating grain and to promote weight gain. Though the drugs must be stopped for a period before slaughter, there is still fear that antibiotics will be passed on to humans, reducing resistance to superbugs. And finally, large-scale animal feeding has been shown to be detrimental to water resources, soil health and human health in the transference of e coli and other diseases. Yes, leaner grass-fed beef is usually more expensive to the consumer. But eating less, but better, beef is good for the planet and worth the cost.

CHAPTER 3

CEVICHE, CEVICHE, CEVICHE

When I was about 10 years old, I watched a well-known chef, Javier Wong, cook for friends. From a cooler, he took a just-caught prime summer flounder. A few cuts, squeezes of lime, slicing of onions and rocoto pepper, and he had created a fantastic ceviche. To me, it was an epiphany — so cool. I remember wishing I could do that someday.

Ceviche is rightfully called the signature dish of Peru, its bright, simple flavors a testament to the Peruvian obsession with freshness. The key to today's cooking is using as few ingredients as possible. Simplicity and speed makes ceviche perfect now especially since classic recipes are supposed to have no more than five ingredients. But this glorious ode to fresh seafood often seems exotic, even scary, to home cooks. We'll pay good money for ceviche in a restaurant, but shy away from making it at home.

Peruvians have known for centuries that the flavors of a dish that combines only fresh fish, lime or lemon juice, and maybe a sprinkling of thinly sliced onion and fresh hot pepper can be astounding. And there's nothing to fear. Follow my directions and your family and friends will rave.

There are many stories about where the word "ceviche" came from. Some say it was brought to Peru and Ecuador by Arab traders, and is derived from the Arabic word, "seibiech," or acidic. Other stories more colorfully say that an English sailor stumbled on a Peruvian eating raw fish with salt and hot peppers on a beach, and when the sailor tasted the dish, he exclaimed "sonabitch," later smoothed to ceviche.

Recipes:
- » Basic Fish Ceviche
- » New England Ceviche
- » Scallop Tiradito
- » Ceviche de Tarwi

63

Ceviche, as we know it with Peruvian lemon or lime as the cooking agent, started after Spaniards brought the Middle Eastern fruit to South America, although pre-Hispanic versions used tumbo, an acidic fruit from the Andes. But ceviche's preparation has always evolved. After Japanese workers immigrated to Peru in the late 19th century, their traditions of eating raw fish as sashimi led to tiradito, or raw fish cut like sashimi and often flavored with soy and other Asian ingredients.

Whatever the evolution of ceviche, it's versatile, easy to make, and impressive. The chief requirement is very fresh fish and good limes or Peruvian lemons. Beyond that, your imagination is your limit! And, remember, the freshest possible fish is a must!

NEW ENGLAND CEVICHE

Being in New England gives you the opportunity to source really fresh seafood, and to make a good ceviche, you will need a super fresh fish. This recipe is basically a traditional Peruvian Ceviche but made with New England seafood.

SERVES 8-10

INGREDIENTS

- » ½ pound fluke (also known as summer flounder)
- » ½ pound lobster meat, cooked
- » ½ pound shucked littleneck clams, or surf or razor clams
- » ½ pound bay scallops, or sea scallops, cut in half
- » 2 red onions, sliced thinly
- » 2 teaspoons aji amarillo paste
- » 2 teaspoons rocoto paste
- » Juice of 20 Key limes or 8 regular limes
- » Sea salt

TO SERVE:
4 ears boiled corn, cut into rounds
4 boiled sweet potatoes, cut into wedges

DIRECTIONS

1. Cut fish and lobster meat into bite-size pieces, and mix fish, clams and scallops together with sliced onions in a large bowl. Season with salt and ajÌ amarillo and rocoto pastes.

2. Toss fish preparation quickly in lime juice. Refresh by adding 8-10 ice cubes, mixing well; removing the ice before the cubes have a chance to melt. Serve ceviche immediately in a deep dish, accompanied by slices of boiled sweet potato and rounds of fresh cooked corn.

BASIC FISH CEVICHE

Classic Peruvian ceviche allows only 5 ingredients: fish, lime, salt, onion and aji (chilies). It's clean, simple and fresh, and does not require a long marinating time. Try to get local fish that have been caught within a day or so of serving.

SERVES 4-6

INGREDIENTS

- » 1 pound fresh summer flounder or wild striped bass filets
- » 1 red onion, sliced very thinly
- » 1/2 teaspoon aji amarillo paste
- » 1/2 teaspoon rocoto paste
- » Juice of 16 Key limes, or 6-8 medium regular limes
- » Sea salt

TO SERVE:
1 boiled ear of corn, cut into rounds
1 boiled sweet potato, cut into wedges

DIRECTIONS

1. Cut fish into bite-size pieces, put in a large bowl. Season with salt, and add ajÌ amarillo and rocoto pastes. Toss fish and pastes quickly, adding lime juice, and then sliced red onion. Add a couple of ice cubes to the bowl to refresh, and mix again.

2. Remove the ice before the cubes have a chance to melt. Serve ceviche immediately in a deep dish, accompanied by slices of boiled sweet potato and rounds of fresh cooked corn.

SCALLOP TIRADITO

This recipe is so simple and so clean that you won't believe the delight from diners. The technique of thinly slicing each scallop is reminiscent of Japanese sashimi. And that's where it started -- Japanese immigrants brought their knife techniques to Peru, leaving behind a seafood tradition that lasts even today.

SERVES 2-4

INGREDIENTS

- » 4 U10* very fresh sea scallops
- » 4 tablespoons freshly squeezed lime juice
- » 2 tablespoons cilantro leaves, chopped
- » 1 garlic clove, chopped fine
- » 1 dollop rocoto paste
- » ½ teaspoon aji amarillo paste
- » Sea salt salt flakes, such as Maras or Maldon

DIRECTIONS

1. Remove the muscle texture attached to the body of the scallop, then cut each scallop horizontally into 3-4 slices. Set out two-four small salad or appetizer plates.

2. Make a sauce by mixing the lime juice with aji amarillo, garlic and cilantro, using an immersion hand blender or a small whisk.

3. Fan out slices of scallop on each plate and pour the lime mixture over them. Add a little dollop of rocoto chili paste, then sprinkle with salt flakes.

10 or fewer scallops to a pound

CEVICHE DE TARWI

Lupini or tarwi beans are nutritious and high in protein. Although in their raw state, they contain alkaloids, the canned or bottled products have been treated to remove those, and need only to be soaked to remove salt. The beans make a vegan alternative to ceviche, and are nutty and delicious. In the region of Ancash is very common to see "Chocherias" where they serve the Tarwi or Chocho Ceviche, aka 'Cevichocho."

71

SERVES 6 AS APPETIZER

INGREDIENTS

- » 4 cups lupini (tarwi) beans, canned
- » 1 large red onion, sliced thin
- » 1 teaspoon salt
- » 4 limes, juiced
- » 1 teaspoon aji amarillo paste
- » 1 bunch cilantro, chopped

DIRECTIONS

1. Drain the canned beans and soak overnight in cold water to remove salt. Keep refrigerated.

2. Place the sliced red onions and 1 teaspoon salt in a large bowl and cover with cold water to reduce the onion's harshness. Let soak for about 5 minutes, then drain and rinse well.

3. Make a dressing by whisking together the lime juice and aji amarillo paste. Combine the dressing with red onions, tarwi beans, and chopped cilantro.

4. Serve immediately

ABOUT TARWI

Tarwi beans, which contain an incredible 40 percent protein that is comparable to animal proteins, are examples of the Andean ingenuity in sourcing nutrition. In large quantities and in raw form, tarwi or chocho can be poisonous because the beans contain alkaloids that can affect the nervous system. Although the alkaloids can be removed by soaking, making the beans palatable and safe for humans, using canned or jarred lupini that have been treated to be safe to eat, is preferable for home cooks..

In the Ancash region of Peru, where the Santa Cruz Lodge is located, native cooks boil these beans all day and then place them in a burlap sack that is submerged in pristine running river water for three days. Boiling the beans removes the alkaloid poisoning and the river water eliminates bitterness. Then the beans are roasted and eaten as a snack. In Peru and Bolivia, they are also ground into flour to make bread or noodles. Dried lupini beans or flour found in stores in the United States have been treated to remove the alkaloids and bitterness.

NORTHERN PERU: THE BIRTHPLACE OF CEVICHE

My mother grew up in northern Peru, where ceviche originated. Because of its proximity to the equator, the climate is dry, warm and sunny, and the predominating flavors are fresh, brightly herbal cilantro and juice from the fragrant, and not very acidic, Peruvian limes.

My great-grandfather, whose surname was Woodman, was from England, and came to Peru to be involved in the cotton and candle industries. The family owned a large amount of land and lived a colonial lifestyle in houses with ornate architecture where afternoon tea was served with a formal protocol – finger sandwiches, table settings, and servants.

Because of the coastal influence, there is a lot of seafood, which my mother's family enjoyed in summers on the beach. Although ceviche is now the flag dish of all of Peru, northern Peru had the first cevicherias. The most important consideration in making ceviche is the freshness of the fish. In the old days, ceviche was normally eaten in the daytime because tradition had it that the fish must be pulled from the ocean that morning; by nightfall, the cevicherias would be closed. Unlike ceviche in Mexico or other places, the seafood is not allowed to sit in marinade for more than a few minutes, making it even more important that the fish be immaculately fresh. There's nothing better on a hot day — chilled ceviche with only onion, lime juice, and hot pepper, accompanied by a cold beer!

CHAPTER 4

QUINOA,
THE WONDER FOOD

Until a decade or so ago, few Americans had heard of quinoa. Now the tiny seed from the goosefoot family is ubiquitous -- the protein-rich darling of the Western diet. Although most diners reaching for a quick and satisfying meal barely know about its 5,000-year history in the Andes, quinoa is a controversial pawn in the tug between health-conscious Americans and the indigenous peoples of South America.

Quinoa may be touted as the trendy healthy grain with the hard-to-pronounce name (keenwah), but for centuries this protein-rich member of the same family as spinach, beets, and amaranth sustained the inhabitants of high country in Peru, Bolivia, and Ecuador. In the sandy soil and high-altitude climate of the Andes where other grains could not take hold, quinoa flourished, giving sustenance to mountain dwellers and inspiration to pottery makers and other craftsmen. Today Peru is one of the largest producers of quinoa. Now, as the demand for quinoa grows, there is fear that the once-humble source of nourishment will be priced out of supply for those who have traditionally eaten it.

In the future, I hope to be able to support a program in the highlands to grow quinoa, sustainably and organically, in ways that will benefit not only those who are nourished by this wondrous seed, but also those who grow it.

Now I'm here to tell you about the deliciousness and amazing versatility of this ancient pseudo-cereal grain. In soups, in salads, in puddings, in drinks, quinoa can add substance and nutrition to almost any course of any meal. Although there are hundreds of varieties and colors in Peru, white, red and black are readily available in the United States and add visual drama to any dish. You'll want to use quinoa in many ways to nourish your family and delight your guests.

Recipes:
- » Quinoa and Pallares Soup
- » Quinoa Crab Cakes
- » Mushroom Quinotto
- » Quinoa and Polenta Square
- » Quinoa Verde
- » Rainbow Quinoa and Tomato Salad
- » Quinoa con Leche

QUINOA CRAB
CAKES

QUINOA CRAB CAKES

Using quinoa in place of bread or cracker crumbs in these crab cakes
gives a pleasing crunch and adds nutritional value to a simple favorite.

SERVES 4

INGREDIENTS

» 3/4 cup cooked white quinoa, chilled
» 1 pound jumbo lump crabmeat
» 4 tablespoons mayonnaise
» 1 teaspoon Worcestershire sauce
» 1 large egg, beaten
» 4 tablespoons unsalted butter
» Serve with Aji Amarillo Aioli (Page 169)

DIRECTIONS

1. Mix cooked quinoa in a bowl with crab. Add mayonnaise,
   Worcestershire sauce, beaten egg, and salt and pepper. Mix
   together gently; then form into 8 patties.

2. Heat butter in a 12-inch heavy skillet over medium heat
   until foam subsides. Then saute crab cakes, turning once,
   until golden brown, about 8 minutes total.

3. Serve with Aji Amarillo Aioli.

QUINOA AND PALLARES SOUP

This hearty soup is easy to make and a satisfying vegetarian meal.

SERVES 4

INGREDIENTS

» 3 tablespoons extra virgin olive oil
» 1 medium white onion, chopped
» 2 medium carrots, peeled and chopped
» 2 celery stalks, chopped
» 3 garlic cloves,minced
» 1 cup diced tomatoes

» 1 cup of white or mixed quinoa, rinsed well in a fine mesh colander
» 4 cups vegetable broth
» 2 cups water
» Salt and pepper to taste
» 2 cups giant Peruvian lima beans, precooked or canned

DIRECTIONS

1. Heat olive oil in a large pot, and when the oil starts to shimmer, add the chopped onions, carrots and celery. Cook, stirring often, until the onion has softened and turns translucent, about 5 to 7 minutes.

2. Add the garlic. Cook for about 1 minute stirring frequently,

3. Add the diced tomatoes and continue cooking for 3 minutes, stirring frequently.

4. Pour in the quinoa, then the broth and water, and season with salt and pepper to your liking. Increase the heat and allow the mixture to come to a boil, then cover the pot and lower the heat to simmer.

5. Cook for 20 minutes, then remove the lid and add the lima beans. Simmer for 8 minutes or more. Adjust seasoning if needed.

MUSHROOM QUINOA "QUINOTTO"

Risotto made with quinoa not only melds Peruvian and Italian cooking styles, but adds the nutritional punch of quinoa. An easy and delicious dish that can accompany meat or fish or stand on its own as a vegetarian entree.

SERVES 4 AS SIDE DISH, 2 AS ENTREE

INGREDIENTS

- » 1 cup white quinoa
- » 3 cups water
- » 2 cups vegetable broth
- » Salt and pepper to taste
- » 1 tablespoon olive oil
- » 1 ½ cups chopped onions
- » 1 garlic clove, pressed
- » 2 portobello mushrooms, 3 crimini mushrooms, 5 large button mushrooms, all chopped
- » 2 teaspoons chopped fresh thyme
- » 2 teaspoons chopped fresh rosemary
- » 1 cup white wine
- » 2 tablespoons butter
- » ¼ cup heavy cream
- » Grated Parmesan cheese, extra virgin olive oil

DIRECTIONS

1. In a medium saucepan, spread quinoa and roast for 2 minutes over high heat tossing continuously. Once quinoa is lightly browned, add 3 cups of water and bring to a boil. Strain the quinoa, discarding the cooking water, and then rinse the quinoa.This process helps eliminate the saponin in quinoa that makes it bitter. Return quinoa to the saucepan. Add vegetable broth, bring to boil, and reduce heat to medium-low. Cover pan, and simmer until broth is absorbed, and quinoa is tender, about 12 minutes.

2. Meanwhile, heat oil in a large skillet over medium-high heat. Add onions and sauté until they begin to brown, about 5 minutes. Add garlic, and saute 30 seconds. Add mushrooms and herbs. Sauté until mushrooms are tender, about 6 minutes. Add wine; cook, stirring, until liquid is reduced and syrupy, about 2 minutes.

3. Mix quinoa with mushroom mixture. Add butter and cream, and cook for 2 minutes more until cream is reduced, stirring continuously. Serve with grated Parmesan cheese and a drizzle of extra virgin olive oil.

QUINOA AND POLENTA SQUARE

When I visited my grandmother, Paulina, she would sometimes prepare polenta the way she learned from her father, Antonio Mungi, an Italian immigrant from Piedmont, Italy. At first, I was not too taken by the idea of eating a puree-like mixture with a "ragu" on top. But after the first two bites one wintry day in Lima, I immediately asked for seconds. I developed the idea of preparing polenta with a quinoa component one day after I had overcooked quinoa. I noticed the texture was a little like polenta, so I mixed some prepared polenta and the soft quinoa to make a polenta square. I seared the squares over high heat, resulting in a delicious side dish.

FOR POLENTA SQUARE

INGREDIENTS

- » 3 ½ cups whole milk
- » 1 cup coarse cornmeal (polenta)
- » 1 cup cooked quinoa
- » ½ cup grated Parmesan cheese
- » Salt and pepper to taste

DIRECTIONS

1. In a medium stock pot simmer 3 ½ cups milk until hot, then add polenta gradually while stirring. Add quinoa and cook for about 3 minutes until the cornmeal starts to thicken and pulls away from the sides of the pot. Remove from heat, and add Parmesan.

2. Pour the polenta-quinoa mixture into a 3-inch deep pan, and let it cool until it hardens. Cut into squares, and sear the squares over medium-high heat in a nonstick skillet until golden on both sides.

QUINOA VERDE

Healthy quinoa is mixed with greens, herbs and other vegetables for a light, but fulfilling, vegan main course. The texture will be similar to risotto.

SERVES 4

INGREDIENTS

- » 3 cups white quinoa
- » 4 1/2 cups water
- » 2 tablespoons extra virgin olive oil
- » 1 cup onion, chopped
- » 4 garlic cloves, chopped
- » ½ cup ají amarillo paste
- » 1 teaspoon turmeric
- » 1 cup cilantro leaves
- » 1 cup spinach leaves
- » 4 cups vegetable stock
- » Salt and pepper
- » 1 red bell pepper, diced
- » 1 cup green peas
- » 1 cup giant Peruvian corn kernels, thawed if frozen
- » 1 cup diced carrots
- » Salsa Criolla (Page 167)

DIRECTIONS

1. In a saucepan, spread out quinoa and roast without oil over medium heat until lightly brown. (This will help enhance the nutty flavor of the quinoa) Add 4 cups of water and bring to a boil, then discard water and rinse the quinoa. Set aside in a bowl.

2. In a medium saucepan, heat oil over medium heat, add the chopped onion and garlic and saute for about 5 minutes. Add quinoa, ají amarillo and turmeric; stir and cook for 8 more minutes.

3. Process cilantro, spinach and ½ cup water in a blender. Add to the saucepan, together with the vegetable stock. Season with salt and pepper, cover tightly, turn the heat to low and cook until quinoa is tender.

4. Add red pepper, peas, corn and carrots to the saucepan, and cook for 5 more minutes. Taste for seasoning. Serve with Salsa Criolla (Page 167)

RAINBOW QUINOA AND PALLARES SALAD

Tri-color quinoa gives this simple salad distinction. It's a great summer lunch dish or a side dish for roast or grilled meats.

SERVES 4-6 AS A SIDE DISH

INGREDIENTS

- » 1 cup rainbow pre-washed quinoa (tri-color blend)
- » 1 large lemon
- » 1 tablespoon chia seeds
- » 2 tablespoons extra virgin olive oil
- » ¾ cup minced red onion
- » ¾ teaspoon kosher salt
- » ¾ teaspoon coarse ground black pepper
- » 1 cup cooked Giant Peruvian lima beans, also called pallares
- » 1 cup cherry or grape tomatoes, cut in half
- » 3 fresh basil leaves, slivered

DIRECTIONS

1. Place the quinoa in a saucepan and roast for a couple of minutes, then add 1 1/2 cups water. Bring to a boil, pour the water out, and add another 1 1/2 cups water and cook for about 10 minutes until al dente. Once quinoa is cooked, drain excess water, and spread out on a sheet pan to cool, then refrigerate.

2. Juice the lemon into a small bowl and add 1 teaspoon of chia seeds. Let the seeds soak for a few minutes. Then add olive oil, whisking to emulsify. Add salt and pepper and whisk again.

3. In a mixing bowl, combine the minced red onion, cherry tomatoes, and lemon dressing. Let stand for 5 minutes, until the onions have softened slightly.

4. Remove quinoa from the refrigerator and mix with the rest of the ingredients. Add the pallares and basil. Adjust salt to taste. Serve cold.

QUINOA CON LECHE

This dessert is similar to Arroz Con Leche. Substituting quinoa for rice adds protein and nutrition while still giving the dessert a delicate creaminess.

SERVES 4

INGREDIENTS

- » 1/2 vanilla bean, split
- » 4 cups whole milk, divided
- » 1 cup white quinoa
- » 5 cups water, divided
- » 1 12-ounce can sweetened condensed milk
- » 2 cinnamon sticks
- » 1 tablespoon lemon zest
- » 2 whole cloves
- » 1/2 cup dried Incan golden berries (optional)
- » Lemon peel, grated cinnamon for garnish

DIRECTIONS

1. In a small saucepan, warm 1/4 cup of the whole milk. Scrape the inside of the vanilla bean into the milk and add the bean to extract the flavor.

2. In a medium saucepan, add the quinoa and 2 cups of water and bring to a boil. Strain the quinoa in a colander and rinse with cold water. Rinse the saucepan and put quinoa back in and add 3 cups of water. Bring the mixture to a boil on high heat, uncovered. After it starts to boil (about 5 minutes), lower the heat to medium and cook for 10 to 12 more minutes or until water has almost evaporated.

3. Then add the remaining 3 ¾ cups whole milk to the quinoa, and stir well to mix. Discard the vanilla bean shell and add vanilla-infused milk, condensed milk, cinnamon sticks, lemon zest and cloves to the quinoa and cook over medium-low heat, stirring often, until it thickens slightly or until desired consistency, about 25 minutes. Add Incan golden berries (Aguaymanto) and stir.

4. Serve in 4 individual glass cups, garnish with a lemon peel and grated cinnamon.

CHAPTER 5

PERUVIAN BOUNTY: POTATOES, BEANS, AND CORN

Walk through markets in Peru, and you'll be astonished at the dozens, even hundreds, of varieties of potatoes, the myriad colors and kinds of dried beans, the displays of corn, of chocolate. The potato aisles alone in the city market of Cuzco, where displays of varieties in colors, shapes and sizes go on and on, dazzle the eye. Dried beans displayed in burlap bags and terracotta containers are equally impressive. Corn, too, ranges from large-kernel to tiny, white to purple to brilliant yellow to many other shades, sizes and varieties. Other stalls show chocolate and raw cacao, which is beginning to gain prominence in Peru as new, exotic strains are found in the Amazonian forests.

To Peruvians, these foods are more than their heritage — they're integral to daily meals. Using them creatively, as might be done in Peru, can add nutrition and incredible flavor to your meals. My grandmother Paulina might have chosen a certain type of corn to serve with a ceviche or stew, used chuño potatoes to thicken a sauce, or found just the right chocolate that one of her sons loved. Today, chefs in the finest restaurants in Lima and elsewhere are doing the same thing, sourcing the bounty of Peru for their exquisite dishes.

Here, we might make a trip to a South American ethnic grocery or search online to source ingredients, expanding our knowledge of the culinary world. In any case, the nutritional value of these staples —- potatoes, beans, and corn —- only adds to their delicious flavors. You'll find these recipes open your eyes and taste buds to a world beyond our borders.

Recipes:
- » Papa Rellena
- » White Chuño Potato Gratin
- » Papa Seca Salad
- » Braised Duck with Huaripampa Beans Tacu Tacu
- » Lomo Saltado with Yellow Potato Gnocchi
- » Tarwi Polpette
- » Cheesecake with Chicha Morada Glaze

PAPA RELLENA

This is a papa rellena that wants to be arancini, a crossover between stuffed potatoes and the Italian stuffed rice balls. Whatever its inspiration, it's delicious. My grandmother's meat filling would have been a little drier than mine, but I've updated and enriched her version by adding porcini and mozzarella.

MAKES 4 STUFFED POTATOES

INGREDIENTS

- » 3 pounds yellow potatoes
- » 3 tablespoons olive oil
- » ¼ cup diced frozen porcini mushrooms, or 1 ounce dried porcini
- » 1/2 cup red onion, finely chopped
- » 1 tablespoon aji amarillo pepper paste.
- » ¼ teaspoon cumin
- » ¼ teaspoon paprika
- » 1 lb pound ground beef
- » ¾ cup beef broth
- » 1 tablespoon tomato paste
- » ¼ cup diced mozzarella
- » 2 hard-boiled eggs, chopped
- » ½ cup of all purpose flour
- » 1 egg, whisked with 1 tablespoon water
- » 1 tablespoon Italian parsley, chopped fine
- » Salt and pepper to taste
- » ½ cup or more canola oil

DIRECTIONS

1. Boil the potatoes in salted water. Cool just enough to handle and peel. Cut into pieces and put through a potato ricer. Season the riced potatoes with salt and pepper.

2. Soak dried porcini in hot water for 10 minutes, then drain and chop. Or if using frozen porcini, cut into cubes. In a small skillet, heat 1 tablespoon olive oil and saute porcini.

3. In a medium saute pan, heat 2 tablespoons olive oil and saute garlic and onion for 5 minutes until softened; then add porcini, aji amarillo, onion, paprika, and cumin, sauteeing until golden brown. Add ground beef and cook for about 6 minutes over high heat. Add beef broth and reserved liquid from soaking porcini and cook for another 15 minutes. Salt and pepper to taste. Set aside and let mixture cool to lukewarm, then add mozzarella and hard boiled eggs.

4. Flour a cutting board or baking sheet. Make four circles, each 6 inches in diameter of the riced potatoes. Make a depression in the center of each circle and with a large spoon, stuff the sauteed ingredients into the depression. Fold the edges of the potatoes over the filling, completely covering the filling. Dip each stuffed potato into the egg wash and then into the flour.

5. Heat an inch of canola oil in a saute pan, and fry each stuffed potato lightly on both sides, until golden. Serve with Salsa Criolla.

TARWI POLPETTE

Because tarwi (or chocho, as the beans are known in the Ancash region) are high in protein, they are excellent substitutes for meat. These croquettes, or meatless meatballs, have as much protein as meat. Also called lupini, dry tarwi beans must be treated to remove alkaloids; jarred lupini in brine must be rinsed.

SERVES 4

INGREDIENTS

- » 1 tablespoon extra virgin olive oil
- » 2 cups vegetable oil
- » 1 garlic clove, finely chopped
- » 1 red onion, finely chopped, divided
- » 1 small bunch parsley, chopped, divided
- » ½ teaspoon aji panca pepper paste (optional)

- » ½ teaspoon black pepper
- » 1 pound canned lupini, rinsed as directed
- » 1 small potato, cut into small cubes
- » ½ cup water
- » ½ cup breadcrumbs
- » 1 large egg, lightly beaten
- » Salt, pepper

DIRECTIONS

1. In a medium saute pan, heat olive oil and 1 tablespoon vegetable oil. Saute garlic, ½ of the red onion, ½ the chopped parsley, and aji panca paste until the garlic is golden. Then add the lupini beans and continue to cook for two minutes. Add the potato cubes, season with black pepper. After 5 minutes, add water. Cook for 30 minutes, continue adding water if needed so the mixture does not dry out or burn.

2. Once cooked, use a large fork and press, leaving some lupini beans whole. Let the mixture cool. Then add breadcrumbs, egg, the rest of the chopped onion and the chopped parsley.

3. Place in a bowl, mix well, and form into small balls. Refrigerate for 15 minutes

4. Using a cast iron Dutch oven or a medium stockpot, heat 2 cups of vegetable oil to 350F and deep fry the polpetti until golden brown

5. Serve with Salsa Criolla (Page 167).

PAPA SECA SALAD

Papa seca are diced potatoes dried in the sun to preserve them. They are integral to Peruvian home cuisine and their slightly nutty flavor adds nuance to a traditional potato salad.

SERVES 4

INGREDIENTS

- » 2 cups of dried Papa Seca
- » ½ cup diced red onion
- » ½ cup diced celery
- » ¼ cup good-quality commercial mayonnaise
- » 3 teaspoons aji panca pepper paste
- » 1 tablespoon minced garlic
- » 2 tablespoons lime juice
- » 3 tablespoons chopped Italian parsley

DIRECTIONS

1. To make potato mixture: Make sure to check the dried papa seca for small stones as they could easily be camouflaged into the mix. Then cover the potatoes with cold water and soak in the refrigerator for about 24 hours. Drain, and in a medium stock pot, cover the potatoes with water, add a pinch of salt, and bring to a boil. Boil the potatoes until barely tender, about 15 minutes, then strain and cool. Chill in the refrigerator.

2. Mix the rest of the ingredients, as if making a typical American potato salad.

3. Slice chilled potatoes and add to mayonnaise mixture. This is a great summer dish to serve chilled with grilled seafood or beef.

BRAISED DUCK
WITH HUARIPAMPA BEANS TACU TACU

Tacu Tacu is a homey Peruvian version of refried rice and beans with a long history. Takuy in Quechua means to mix, and the dish made by indigenous peoples who combined rice and beans was probably refined by African slaves brought over by Spaniards in the 16th century. Tacu tacu makes a superb base for peppery braised duck, elevating the homey into a showy centerpiece.

SERVES 4

INGREDIENTS

- » 2 cups cooked Peruvian lima beans
- » ½ cup chicken stock, divided
- » 2 cups cooked white rice
- » 2 teaspoons olive oil plus 1 tablespoon to brush pan

DIRECTIONS

1. In a blender or food processor, puree 1 cup of the beans with ¼ cup chicken stock. In a bowl, mix the pureed beans and the remaining 1 cup whole beans with the rest of the chicken stock, the rice and 2 tablespoons olive oil.

2. Brush a non-stick saute pan with olive oil, heat over medium heat, and add the mixture, patting evenly with a spatula. Let the heat create a crust on the outside (the rice will get golden crisp) then turn to cook the other side. The result should be crisp outside and moist and a little soft inside.

89

FOR PANCA PEPPER BRAISED DUCK LEG

INGREDIENTS

- » 2 tablespoons canola oil
- » 4 duck legs, excess fat removed
- » 2 large white onions, chopped
- » 2 garlic cloves, chopped
- » 3 teaspoons panca pepper
- » Salt, pepper to taste
- » 3 ½ cups chicken stock

DIRECTIONS

1. Preheat the oven to 350 degrees. In a braising pan with a lid that can go into the oven, heat canola oil over medium heat. Season duck legs with salt and pepper, and add to the braising pan, skin side down. Flip when the skin side is golden brown. Move legs to one side and add onions, garlic and panca paste to pan; cook for about 10 minutes over medium heat. Add chicken stock, bring to a boil.

2. Spread legs evenly over the pan. Cover and place in a preheated oven. Bake for about one hour adding more stock if the mixture is too dry.

TO SERVE

Cut the tacu tacu into four pieces and place on plates. Place a duck leg on top of each piece, drizzling with pan juices. Fried ripe plantain rings can be served on top.

WHITE CHUÑO POTATO AU GRATIN
WITH GRUYERE AND HUACATAY

Chuño is a freeze-dried potato from the Peruvian Andes. Although it is normally used to thicken soups, I have experimented and made a delicious "au gratin."

91

SERVES 8 AS A SIDE DISH

INGREDIENTS

- » 1 pound white dried chuño potatoes
- » 4 ounces unsalted butter
- » 1 tablespoon huacatay leaves
- » 2 shallots, diced
- » 1 sprig of thyme

- » 1 quart heavy cream
- » ½ pound Gruyere cheese, diced
- » ¼ pound Parmesan cheese, grated
- » 5 tablespoons breadcrumbs
- » Salt and pepper to taste

DIRECTIONS

1. Soak chuño potatoes in cold water in the refrigerator for 24 hours. Boil about 1 ½ hours until barely tender. These will have the texture of yucca and won't soften like other potatoes. Chill for at least an hour, and slice into thinnest slices possible without breaking the potatoes. In a separate saucepan, melt butter, and over very low heat, add huacatay, shallots and thyme, allowing the herbs to flavor the butter. Add heavy cream at the end. Allow to cool to room temperature.

2. In a mixing bowl, place the sliced potatoes and mix with the cream mixture, diced gruyere and all but 2 tablespoons of Parmesan. Pour into a buttered gratin pan. Sprinkle the top with the extra Parmesan and breadcrumbs.

3. Cover with aluminum foil and bake in the oven for 30 minutes. Remove the foil and bake 5 to 10 minutes more to create a crust. Let it sit for 8-10 minutes so that the cheese and cream settle and cool. Cut into squares and reheat as needed.

LOMO SALTADO
WITH YELLOW POTATO GNOCCHI

This Peruvian classic is part of the chifa craze started after Chinese immigration in the late 1800s. Seasoned with soy sauce and vinegar, the rich, meaty sauce is balanced with potato gnocchi. The recipe uses Papa Amarilla, native to Peru. However, Yukon gold potatoes are a good substitute. It's a happy marriage of Peruvian chifa traditions and Italian cooking.

92

SERVES 4

—————— FOR LOMO SALTADO ——————

INGREDIENTS

» 2 tablespoons canola oil
» 2 4-oz pieces of beef tenderloin, cut into 2 inch cubes
» 1 teaspoon Peruvian garlic paste
» 1 teaspoon aji amarillo
» 2 teaspoons soy sauce
» 2 tablespoons sherry vinegar

» 1 tablespoon Worcester sauce
» 1 teaspoon dry oregano
» ½ cup of cherry or grape red tomatoes, halved
» ¼ large red onion, sliced in thick rounds
» 1 tablespoon chopped parsley or chopped chives

DIRECTIONS

1. This dish is best done in a wok; if not available, use a large saute pan. The flavor of the dish comes from the high-heat reaction between the sauteed meat, and vinegar, soy, and Worcester sauce, done as a stir fry.

2. First heat the pan until very hot, add the oil and quickly add meat, garlic and aji amarillo. Then quickly add the onion and tomatoes, saute a few minutes until meat is just cooked through.

3. Mix soy sauce, sherry vinegar and Worcester sauce in a small bowl. Add to a wok or saute pan along with the tomatoes and onion. Sautee quickly. The meat must be medium rare and the onion should still have a crunch. Sprinkle with parsley or chopped chives before serving.

—————— FOR GNOCCHI ——————

INGREDIENTS

- » 2 large Yukon gold potatoes
- » 2 cups of 00 flour*
- » 1 teaspoon salt or to taste
- » 1 egg, lightly beaten
- » 1 tablespoon olive oil or melted butter

DIRECTIONS

1. Preheat the oven to 375 F. Very lightly oil a rimmed baking sheet and place potatoes on it. Bake in the oven for an hour or until very tender when pierced with a knife. Cool slightly, peel and then mashed with a potato masher or press through a potato ricer.

2. In a large, flat-bottomed bowl or on a wooden board, spread half the flour in a circle; sprinkle salt over flour. Spread mashed potatoes over the flour and then cover with ½ cup of the flour. Drizzle the beaten egg over the potato-flour mixture. Using a bench scraper, gently fold the flour and potatoes together, just until the flour, potato and egg is mixed; do not knead or overwork or gnocchi will be tough.

3. Shape gnocchi dough into a long rope, and cut with a bench scraper or knife into ½-inch pieces. Place on parchment paper sprinkle with flour and freeze.

4. Bring a large pot of water to boil adding salt then the gnocchi. Gnocchi will be ready when floating, carefully remove them, making sure they are drained, toss with the lomo saltado mix in the wok.

CHEESECAKE
WITH CHICHA MORADA GLAZE

America's idea of a cheesecake can be rich, sweet, and in the end, boring. This version uses the classic template but adds the color and flavor of chicha morada (purple corn) with spices to give cheesecake a Latin American sophistication.

94 **SERVES 8 - 10**

—————————— FOR CHEESECAKE ——————————

INGREDIENTS FILLING

- » 1 ½ cup graham cracker crumbs
- » 2 tablespoons sugar
- » 5 ½ tablespoons unsalted butter, melted
- » ½ teaspoon salt
- » 4 large eggs, at room temperature and separated
- » 3 tablespoons flour
- » ½ teaspoon salt
- » 1 ½ cups sugar plus 3 tablespoons
- » 1 ½ pounds cream cheese, room temperature
- » 4 large eggs, at room temperature and separated
- » 1 ⅓ cups sour cream
- » 1 teaspoon vanilla extract

DIRECTIONS

Preheat oven to 300 degrees F

1. Make the crust by combining the crumbs, melted butter and sugar. Lightly spray or coat a 9-inch springform pan with oil. Then press the crumb mixture into the pan, covering the bottom and a few inches up the sides.

1. Lightly mix the egg yolks with a fork to combine.

3. Using a standard mixer or a very heavy hand-held mixer, whip the cream cheese until fluffy. Add flour, salt, 1 ½ cup sugar, and egg yolks, and beat until smooth.

4. Add the sour cream and vanilla and beat until smooth.

5. In a separate bowl, using clean beaters, whip the egg whites until foamy. Begin to add the sugar until egg whites are stiff but not dry.

6. Gently fold the egg whites into the cream cheese mixture, using a spatula. Do not beat.

7. Turn into a prepared pan with crust. Smooth top.

8. Place the springform pan on top of a sturdy cookie sheet or half sheet pan. Bake in a 300-degree oven for 1 hour and 20 minutes. Turn the oven off and cool in the oven for another hour. Remove and allow to cool completely before refrigerating overnight. Top may crack, which is normal.

CHICHA MORADA SAUCE

INGREDIENTS

» 1 (15-ounce) bag of dried purple corn
» 8 cups of water
» 2 cinnamon sticks
» 4 whole cloves
» Peels from ½ pineapple
» 1 teaspoon cornstarch, dissolved in 1 ½ teaspoons cold water
» 1 cup sugar

DIRECTIONS

1. Remove kernels from corn cob and place both in a large stockpot with water, cinnamon sticks, cloves and the pineapple peels. Heat over high heat until boiling, then reduce to medium-low and simmer for 45 minutes. When it has been reduced to about 1 ½ cup of liquid, strain the corn and cobs and reserve the liquid.

2. Remove the liquid mixture from the heat and mix in the sugar; add cornstarch for texture.

3. Cool and serve with cheesecake.

POTATO MAGIC

Potatoes were first cultivated almost 8,000 years ago in Peru. According to folklore, when ancient founders of the Inca empire emerged from Lake Titicaca, the sun god Viracocha taught them to grow potatoes. To this day in the Andes, farmers cultivate hundreds of varieties.

The International Potato Center in Lima has documented more than 4,000 types indigenous to Peru, some that are traded only in local markets. Besides the ways that we use potatoes —boiled, mashed, fried, in gratins, in soups and stews — Peruvians cultivate special types of potatoes that are meant to be freeze-dried, dehydrated and stored. In a process developed before the Incan empire, potatoes are allowed to freeze for three nights in the high, cold Andean air. Then they are washed in cold river pools and left to dry in the sun. The result is chuño, a freeze-dried, dehydrated product that can be kept for months or even years, and also can be used as a thickener.

My grandmother Paulina and many other cooks I know in Peru, including those in high-end, gourmet restaurants, use chuño in soups, stews, and other dishes. Sometimes they are added for special texture or for the nutty taste. Other times, they are used for their thickening properties. In all cases, chuño, which can be purchased in South American specialty groceries in the United States or mail-ordered, must be rehydrated by soaking in water, much as you would soak dried beans before cooking.

Although far from the abundance found in Peru, American groceries and farmers markets are beginning to offer more varieties of potatoes. Far from just a staple, the potato offers nutrients and vitamins as well as a window into a fascinating history.

CHAPTER 6

PAICHE: A LINK TO THE FUTURE OF SEAFOOD?

P aiche on the menu always elicits questions, causing diners to pause and question the waiter: What is it? Where is it from? What does it taste like? Our waiters are always eager to describe this magnificent fresh-water fish that can weigh as much as 400 pounds and reach more than 10 feet in length in the wild. On the plate, the firm texture and mild flavor of paiche belies the almost mythical properties of the Amazonian behemoth that breathes through lungs and can slither like a snake on dry ground.

But there's another component to the paiche legend: It might well be a key player in the sustainable future of seafood. The meat of the paiche, delicate and delicious, is just beginning to be treasured in the United States. In Peru and elsewhere, efforts to raise these fish in clean water, and through nonpolluting and sustainable methods, give hope that paiche can help supply us with a reliable source of protein.

Paiche is popular with diners. However, it can be problematic finding a source of paiche that can be imported into the United States at reasonable prices. By Peruvian law, each fish must be certified as to origin, date of capture, and other details. Although wild paiche is sold to restaurants in Lima, they cannot be exported. By working with companies that sustainably raise paiche in captivity, my goal is to make sure my customers can experience this delicious fish.

Recipes:
- » Cancha-Crusted Paiche with Aji Amarillo Buttermilk Sauce
- » Paiche al Acqua Pazza Peruviana
- » Grilled Paiche with Huacatay Chimichurri
- » Pistachio-Crusted Paiche with Pisco Saffron Butter Sauce
- » Paiche Milanese

CANCHA-CRUSTED PAICHE
WITH AJI AMARILLO BUTTERMILK SAUCE

SERVES 4

INGREDIENTS

- » 2 cups roasted cancha corn
- » Salt and pepper to taste
- » 4 paiche filets, 6 ounces each
- » 3 eggs
- » 1 ¼ cup olive oil, divided
- » 2 cups buttermilk
- » 1 tablespoon Italian flat parsley, chopped
- » ½ large red onion, diced
- » 2 teaspoons aji amarillo paste
- » 4 cups baby spinach
- » ¼ cup white wine vinegar
- » 1 cup fried chickpeas*

DIRECTIONS

1. In a blender or food processor, finely grind the roasted corn, and season with salt and pepper.

2. On a cutting board, put paiche pieces between plastic wrap, and using a meat tenderizer or mallet, flatten each piece into a Milanese-style cutlet. Beat 3 eggs lightly, season with salt and pepper. Place ground cancha on a sheet pan or rimmed cookie sheet. Dip the paiche pieces in the egg wash, and then cover them with the cancha crumbs. Set aside in the refrigerator for 35-45 minutes.

3. In a medium-size bowl, mix buttermilk, chopped parsley, red onion and aji amarillo, and refrigerate. Whisk remaining ¼ cup olive oil and vinegar together for a vinaigrette.

4. In a high-sided saute pan or Dutch oven, heat 1 cup of oil to 350 degrees, using a thermometer to test. Fry the fish until the crumb is golden brown.

5. To serve, place 3 tablespoons of cold buttermilk sauce on the bottom of a shallow serving bowl. Put hot, crispy paiche cutlet on top, and garnish with spinach, fried chickpeas, and a drizzle of the vinaigrette. Repeat with 3 other cutlets. Heat 2 teaspoons of canola oil. Add drained chickpeas, and turn frequently until golden.

*To fry chickpeas, heat a nonstick frying pan, put 2 teaspoons of canola

PAICHE AL ACQUA PAZZA PERUVIANA
WITH CLAMS

This simple fish dish highlights the delicate flavor of paiche contrasted with the sea salt tastes of the clams. It's easy to do for weeknight dinner, yet fancy enough for company.

102

SERVES 4

INGREDIENTS CRUST

- » 4 paiche filets, 6-ounce portions
- » Salt, pepper to taste
- » 2 tablespoons extra virgin olive oil
- » 4 garlic cloves, minced
- » 8 fresh clams

- » 1 tablespoon aji amarillo paste
- » 1 small can Italian cherry tomatoes, 14.1 ounces (or substitute 10 small fresh cherry tomatoes cut in half)
- » ⅓ cup water
- » 1 tablespoon chopped parsley

DIRECTIONS

1. Season filets with salt and pepper
2. Heat a large saute pan, and add olive oil and garlic; saute until garlic is golden, 1-2 minutes. Add fish and cook for about 1 minute on each side, not allowing the garlic to burn.
3. Place clams carefully around filets as they contain liquid and can bubble up. Stir in aji amarillo puree, cherry tomatoes, and water. Simmer for about 10 minutes, adding more salt and pepper to taste, until clams open.
4. Plate filets and two clams each on four plates. Sprinkle with parsley before serving. Serve with toasted bread.

PISTACHIO CRUSTED PAICHE
WITH PISCO SAFFRON BUTTER SAUCE

This elegant dish combines the punch of Pisco, Peru's beloved brandy, with the crunch and bright color of pistachios for a dinner-party-worthy centerpiece.

SERVES 4

INGREDIENTS CRUST

- » 4 tablespoons unsalted pistachios, chopped coarsely
- » 4 tablespoons breadcrumbs
- » Salt and pepper
- » 4 paiche filet portions, 6- to 8-ounces each
- » 2 tablespoons olive oil

DIRECTIONS

1. Season the breadcrumbs with salt and pepper. Mix breadcrumbs and chopped pistachios.

2. Preheat the oven to 350 degrees. Pour olive oil into a large saute pan that can go into the oven. Heat until oil is shimmering. Add paiche filets. Sear one side.

3. Sprinkle pistachio mixture on top of the filets, pressing down to adhere the mixture. Place the pan in the oven for 10 minutes.

4. Remove pan from oven while heating broiler. Under a medium high broiler, broil the fish until the crust is golden brown, about 3 minutes or so. Watch to prevent burning.

5. Serve with saffron sauce, and sauteed spinach and roasted potatoes. Sauce (Page 102)

GRILLED PAICHE WITH HUACATAY CHIMICHURRI

SERVES 4

——— FOR PAICHE ———

INGREDIENTS

- » 4 paiche filets, 6 ounces each portion
- » 3 tablespoons extra virgin olive oil
- » Salt and Pepper

DIRECTIONS

1. Season paiche pieces with salt and pepper to taste. Coat with olive oil.

2. Make sure the grill is very hot. Grill the fish for about 4 to 5 minutes, turning once, depending on the thickness of the piece.

——— HUACATAY CHIMICHURRI ———

INGREDIENTS

- » ⅓ cup red wine vinegar
- » 2 garlic cloves, peeled and minced
- » ¾ teaspoon dried crushed red chilies
- » 1½ teaspoon ground cumin
- » ½ teaspoon salt
- » 2 tablespoon dried oregano
- » ⅓ cup frozen or fresh huacatay leaves, minced
- » 1 cup fresh Italian parsley, finely chopped
- » 2 tablespoons dried oregano
- » ½ cup olive oil

Combine vinegar, minced garlic, crushed red chilies, cumin and salt in a small bowl, and let stand for 8 minutes. Stir in huacatay, parsley, and oregano. Using a fork, whisk in oil. Let it stand for 15 minutes. Use a small spoon to drizzle over grilled paiche as soon as it comes off the grill.

PISTACCHIO CRUSTED PAICHE

FOR THE SAFFRON SAUCE

INGREDIENTS CRUST

- » ½ cup chopped shallots
- » ¼ scant cup Pisco
- » 1 teaspoon saffron threads
- » 2 tablespoons heavy cream
- » 8 ounces unsalted butter, cold and cut into cubes
- » 1 teaspoon fresh lemon juice
- » Salt and pepper

DIRECTIONS

1. Put shallots and Pisco in a small heavy pot, turn the temperature to medium-high, bring to a boil for about 2 to 3 minutes. Remove the shallots with a slotted spoon.

2. Turn down the heat to medium and add saffron, then heavy cream. Add the cold butter cubes one by one, whisking them into the cream mixture. After the butter is incorporated and the sauce is smooth, add lemon juice and salt and pepper to taste.

PAICHE MILANESE

SERVES 4

INGREDIENTS

» 4 paiche filets, 6 ounces each
» 2 eggs, extra large
» 1 ½ cup breadcrumbs
» 1 tablespoon fresh rosemary, chopped
» 1 tablespoon fresh thyme, chopped,
» 2 teaspoons lemon zest
» Salt, pepper to taste
» ½ cup olive oil
» ¼ cup chopped parsley

Optional : Arugula or mixed green salad, lemon vinaigrette

DIRECTIONS

1. Place paiche filet on a sturdy cutting board. Place a large piece of plastic wrap on top of filets, and using a meat tenderizer hammer or the bottom of a small saute pan, flatten the fish until about 1-inch thick.

2. In a medium bowl, beat eggs lightly. In a separate bowl, mix the breadcrumbs with the herbs and lemon zest. Spread the mixture out on a sheet pan.

3. Dip paiche filets in the beaten egg, and then dredge in breadcrumbs, coating completely.

4. Heat olive oil. Over medium heat, saute the fish filets in oil for five minutes on one side. Turn and saute for 2 minutes on the other side until golden brown and fish is cooked through. Do not overcook.

5. Sprinkle filets with parsley. Serve with optional salad and wedges of lemon.

PAICHE AND SUSTAINABILITY

Paiche are part of an ancient group of freshwater fish that once were found all over the planet. But because paiche breathe through lungs and need to rise to the surface for air, they became easy targets for fishermen. By the 1960s, fresh and salted paiche, which had fed generations of Amazonian, became a rare treat.

Wild paiche are making a recovery in parts of Peru, where they are protected. They are also farmed, and in summer 2018, we visited Pucallpa, Peru, near the Amazonian jungle. The paiche, raised in ponds and fed a carefully balanced diet, are transported overnight to the finest Lima restaurants under controlled cold-chain conditions to keep them as fresh as possible. Formerly Taranta and now Tambo benefit from this cultivation and quality control. Now paiche is sometimes available at groceries and specialty fish stores.

CHAPTER 7

FRUITFUL PERU: UNUSUAL FRUITS AND WHAT TO DO WITH THEM

My grandfather Enrique Duarte was truly a gourmet. He savored every meal, had specific times and dishware for each meal, and even carried his portable kit to make Chifa (Peruvian Chinese dishes) by the roadside when he traveled. Enrique was adamant about eating fruit every day, usually first thing in the morning, for its health benefits. There is such a wide variety of fruits in Peru that my grandfather had his pick. His day might start with figs or dates, some tiny plantains or bananas, or even intensely flavorful native strawberries in season.

For me, like my grandfather, Peru has always been a wonderland of fruit. Enrique passed on to me his love of chirimoya (also called custard apple). It's still one of my favorites, with its creamy texture and a slightly acidic tinge to its sweetness. The fruit is very healthful with lots of essential vitamins, antioxidants and minerals.

Peruvians love mangoes -- Peruvian mangoes have the very best flavor, at least that's what Peruvians think. Other fruits such as granadillas, guavas, melons, and cape gooseberries are found in many tropical or subtropical zones. But fruits such as lucuma (often called egg fruit), camu camu, pacay (ice cream bean), tumbo (banana passionfruit) and pepino dulce (sweet cucumber) are native to only a few countries in South America. As well as vitamins and flavor, many of them have other important medicinal properties.

In this abundance of fruits, seasonality is very important. My best memories of my grandmother's house were of the intoxicating scent of strawberries when she made jam. The whole house smelled of them for that brief period when the berries were ripe.

Recipes:
- » Seared Tuna with Incan Golden Berry (also called Cape Gooseberries) Caponata
- » Passion Fruit Tiradito or Ceviche
- » Lucuma and Duck Confit Ravioli
- » Pecan-Crusted Pork Tenderloin, with Pisco-Infused Prune Sauce
- » Cornish Hen Stuffed with Pisco-infused Fruit
- » Incan Golden Berry Bread Pudding
- » Guavannolis

111

In Peru, fruit is used in desserts. Lucuma, chirimoya, and other fruits are used to flavor ice cream, but fruits are also used in many other ways, in savory dishes as well as sweet, and for healthful properties or in home remedies. Not all of these fruits are available in the United States, but more and more are being introduced here. In this chapter, I investigate how fruit can enhance every diet, and how to find substitutes when necessary.

SEARED TUNA
WITH INCAN GOLDEN BERRY CAPONATA

Sashimi quality tuna is recommended for this dish, an adaptation of a traditional Sicilian caponata with Peruvian ingredients. Incan golden berries, also called Cape gooseberries, stand in for golden raisins and add wonderfully sweet-tart flavors. And the cacao gives the caponata an unusual complexity.

SERVES 6-8

INGREDIENTS

- » ½ cup plus 4 tablespoons olive oil, divided
- » 2 pounds small eggplants, cut into 1-inch cubes
- » 1 large yellow onion, chopped
- » 1 celery stick, chopped
- » 2 cloves garlic, finely chopped
- » 3 tablespoons tomato paste, dissolved in ¼ cup water
- » 5 medium tomatoes, peeled, seeded and diced
- » ¼ cup water
- » ½ cup pitted and chopped green olives
- » ½ cup Incan golden berries
- » ¼ cup salt-packed capers, rinsed and drained
- » 1/3 cup white wine vinegar
- » 2 tablespoons brown sugar
- » 2 teaspoons best-quality Peruvian cocoa powder, sifted
- » ¼ cup shredded fresh basil
- » 2 tablespoons pine nuts, toasted
- » 4 tuna steaks, 4 ounces each
- » Salt and pepper to taste

114

DIRECTIONS

1. In a large size saute pan, add 2 tablespoons of olive oil and fry the eggplant cubes, tossing occasionally, until browned, about 5 minutes.

2. Add the onion and celery, and season with salt and freshly ground black pepper. Saute, stirring often, add 2 more tablespoons of olive oil, until the vegetables begin to brown, about 6 minutes.

3. Add the finely chopped garlic and cook 3 minutes more. Lower the heat to medium and add the tomato paste mixed with water and cook, stirring, until caramelized and almost evaporated.

4. Add the diced tomatoes and 1/4 cup water and simmer over low heat for 5 minutes.

5. Add the olives, white wine vinegar, golden berries, capers, brown sugar, and Peruvian cocoa powder into the mixture and continue to cook. Stir occasionally and cook for an additional 5 minutes. If the mixture appears too dry, you can add ¼ cup of water.

6. Meanwhile, season tuna steaks on both sides with salt and pepper. Heat 2-3 tablespoons of olive oil in a large skillet. Saute the tuna, browning lightly on each side. Cut into half and serve alongside goldenberry caponata.

PASSION FRUIT TIRADITO OR CEVICHE

Passion fruit stands in for lemon to cure or "cook" the scallops. This brightly-flavored, slightly acidic dish would be perfect as an appetizer, especially if offered as part of several ceviches.

SERVES 6 AS PART OF APPETIZER SPREAD

INGREDIENTS

- » 6 U-10 very fresh dry scallops or ½ lb very fresh Nantucket bay scallops
- » 6 tablespoons passion fruit concentrate (maracuya)
- » ¼ cup cilantro, chopped
- » 2 teaspoons aji amarillo paste
- » 2-4 teaspoons rocoto paste
- » Sea salt salt flakes, such as Trapanese or Maldon

DIRECTIONS

1. Remove the muscle texture attached to the body of each scallop; then thinly slice each scallop horizontally into 3 slices. If using small bay scallop, slice in half.

2. Make a maracuya sauce by whisking by hand the passion fruit concentrate with aji amarillo, and chopped cilantro. (Do not use an electric blender in order to preserve the texture of the passion fruit.)

3. Place 3 slices of scallop on each of 6 plates and pour passion fruit sauce over the scallops. Add a little dollop of rocoto chili paste on the scallop slices, then sprinkle with salt flakes.

For another version, cut summer flounder or other thin fish filets into squares, and proceed with passion fruit sauce.

LUCUMA AND DUCK CONFIT RAVIOLI
WITH SAGE BROWN BUTTER SAUCE

Although lucuma is fruit, it is not very sweet, and this recipe shows off the fruit's versatility. Its creamy texture and flavor mix well with savory duck confit for these delectable raviolis. These are rich and need only a simple butter sauce with herbs to set them off.

SERVES 4 (ABOUT 20 RAVIOLIS)

INGREDIENTS

- » 3 confit duck legs
- » 2 tablespoons extra virgin olive oil
- » 1 cup lucuma pulp
- » ¼ onion, diced
- » 2 garlic cloves, minced
- » Salt, pepper to taste
- » 1/4 cup chicken or vegetable stock
- » 2 tablespoons butter
- » ¼ cup grated Parmesan cheese
- » ½ cup mascarpone, softened
- » ½ cup breadcrumbs

DIRECTIONS

1. Shred meat from 3 confit legs; it should be a fine shred. In a small saute pan over medium high heat, combine duck meat, olive oil, onion and garlic and cook until onion and garlic are golden brown, about 8 minutes. Add salt and pepper to taste. Add ¼ cup of chicken stock and butter and cook until liquid is reduced to half; set aside to cool.

2. In a large bowl, mix lucuma pulp, duck mixture, Parmesan cheese, and mascarpone, adding breadcrumbs to thicken to a consistency that can be placed into a pastry bag or holds shape on a spoon.

RAVIOLI

INGREDIENTS

- » 2 ½ cup unbleached flour, or OO flour
- » 3 eggs, cold
- » ½ cup cool water
- » ½ cup grated Parmesan

DIRECTIONS

1. Place liquid ingredients in a food processor; mix for a few seconds.

2. Add 1 ½ cups flour and process for a few minutes. Then add the rest of the flour, ½ cup at a time. If sticky to touch, add ¼ cup more flour, a tablespoon at a time.

3. Turn dough onto a wooden board, and dust with flour. Cut into four to six pieces and flatten each piece. Cover each piece with plastic wrap and let rest at least 30 minutes to an hour.

4. Using a long, thin rolling pin or a hand-cranked pasta machine, roll dough until thin enough to see your hand through. Keep the rest of the dough covered until ready to roll out.

5. Using a ravioli cutter, mark sections on one sheet of pasta dough. Pipe or spoon a teaspoonful of duck/lucuma mixture on each square.

6. Roll out another piece of dough. Place over the first and filling and then form the ravioli using a ravioli cutter. The pressure of the cutter should seal the edges to keep the filling in. Repeat with the rest of the dough and filling.

7. Bring a large pot of well-salted water to a boil. Drop ravioli into boiling water, about 8 at a time. When they rise to the surface, remove with a skimmer or slotted spoon to a heated bowl. Repeat until all 20 are cooked.

8. Drizzle ravioli with sage butter sauce, sprinkle with chopped pistachios, and divide among heated serving bowls.

LUCUMA AND DUCK CONFIT RAVIOLI

—— THYME BROWN BUTTER SAUCE ——

INGREDIENTS

» 4 tablespoons butter, cut into cubes
» 1 small clove garlic, minced
» 2 teaspoons fresh thyme leaves
» ¼ cup chopped pistachios (optional)

DIRECTIONS

1. Heat a small saucepan. Add butter, letting it melt over low temperatures, and then continue to cook slowly until butter turns golden brown. Add garlic and thyme and continue to cook until butter is nut-brown.

FINISHING

Divide ravioli among 4 shallow pasta bowls. Drizzle with Thyme Brown Butter Sauce, grated Parmesan, and a few drops of extra virgin olive oil. Top with a sprig of thyme.

CORNISH HEN STUFFED
WITH PISCO-INFUSED FRUIT

Dried fruit gets a boost from Peru's Pisco, a fortified brandy. This delectable main course is just right for a romantic dinner for two. The recipe could be doubled or even tripled for company.

SERVES 2

INGREDIENTS

» ½ cup mixed dried fruit, such as Cape gooseberries (golden berries), cranberries, currants, chopped figs,chopped apricots and chopped dried apples
» ½ cup Pisco
» 1 ½ pound Cornish hen

» 2 tablespoon butter, softened, divided
» Salt, pepper to taste
» ¼ cup cornbread stuffing mix
» 1 sprig thyme, only leaves
» 2 large garlic cloves, peeled

DIRECTIONS

1. Place dried fruit in a glass bowl, cover with Pisco and soak for 1 day. Drain.

2. Preheat the oven to 400 degrees.

3. To prepare the stuffing, combine 1 tablespoon of softened butter, cornbread mix, and thyme in a medium-sized bowl. Season the mixture with salt and pepper to taste. Then, mix in the soaked dried fruit.

4. Clean the interior cavity of the hen and fill it with the stuffing mixture. Tie the hen's legs together using kitchen twine.

5. In a cast iron pan or other ovenproof skillet, place the bird in the center, rub with the remaining softened butter, and sprinkle with salt and pepper. Add garlic cloves. Cover the pan with aluminum foil, and place in the oven.

6. Bake for about 30 minutes. Carefully remove the foil. Then continue to roast for 20-25 more minutes until golden brown. Internal temperature should reach 180 degrees.

7. Allow to rest for 10 minutes before cutting in half or carving for serving.

PECAN-CRUSTED PORK TENDERLOIN
WITH PISCO-INFUSED PRUNE SAUCE

This is a riff on a classic dish, adding a pecan-herb crust, and with Peru's favorite brandy flavoring a prune sauce. It's showy enough for company, yet simple to make.

SERVES 4

INGREDIENTS

» 6 prunes
» ½ cup Pisco
» 3 cups pecans
» 2 cloves garlic
» 1 tablespoon thyme leaves
» 3 fresh sage leaves
» 4 pork tenderloins, 6- to 8-ounce each
» 4 tablespoons olive oil, divided, plus extra to film roasting pan
» Salt and pepper, to taste
» 1 1/2 cups flour
» 5 tablespoons unsalted butter, divided
» 2 garlic cloves, crushed
» ½ cup chicken stock

DIRECTIONS

1. Marinate the prunes in the Pisco for 1 hour.

2. Put pecans, garlic, thyme and sage in a food processor and process until pecans are finely chopped. Add salt and pepper to taste.

3. Brush the tenderloins with 2 tablespoons of olive oil, and sprinkle with salt and pepper. On a rimmed cookie sheet or sheet pan, spread the pecan mixture and the flour, mixing together. Coat the tenderloins, pressing lightly so the pecans coat the whole surface of the loin. Refrigerate for about 35 minutes. Preheat the oven to 350 degrees.

4. Add 2 tablespoons butter and 2 tablespoons oil to a large saute pan and melt butter over medium-high heat. When the mixture is sizzling hot, sear the pork, gently turning so that it is golden brown on all sides. Don't worry if some of the nut-flour mixture comes off in the pan. Wipe out the pan.

5. Lightly film a baking dish with olive oil, and place the tenderloins in it. Set the saute pan aside but do not clean it. Roast the pork in the preheated oven for 20-25 minutes, or until a meat thermometer registers 155-160°F.

6. Meanwhile, make the Pisco prune sauce. Drain the marinated prunes, reserving Pisco. In the saute pan, add 2 tablespoons olive oil, crushed garlic and prunes, and heat over low heat to soften garlic and release flavor.

7. Slowly add remaining butter and reserved Pisco over low heat, stirring constantly so that the butter is incorporated and the mixture doesn't flame. Then add chicken stock, and season with salt and pepper to taste. Simmer until the sauce is reduced by half.

8. Serve with mashed purple Peruvian potatoes or roasted fingerling potatoes and sauteed kale.

121

INCAN GOLDEN BERRY BREAD PUDDING

A classic bread pudding recipe with a delightfully Peruvian twist. Golden berries are high in fiber, vitamins and minerals that can boost immune systems. Infused in pisco infused with sun-dried peaches or aged rum, they are a delightful alternative to raisins. The white chocolate sauce is a decadent flourish.

SERVES 4-6

INGREDIENTS

» 2 cups whole milk
» 2 tablespoons unsalted butter, plus more for greasing pan
» 1 vanilla bean, split lengthwise
» ⅓ cup sugar
» ½ loaf sweet egg bread such as brioche, cut into 2.5-inch cubes (about 5 to 6 cups)
» 2 eggs, beaten
» ½ cup dried Incan golden berries
» 3 tablespoons of huesillo-infused* Pisco or aged rum
» ½ cup heavy cream
» ½ cup white chocolate, chopped

DIRECTIONS FOR PUDDING

1. Heat oven to 350 degrees. In a small saucepan over low heat, warm milk, and add butter, split vanilla bean and sugar. Do not let the mixture come to a boil. Continue cooking just until butter melts; cool. Meanwhile, butter a 4- to 6-cup baking dish and fill it with the bread cubes, mixing in the white chocolate and golden berries.

2. Add eggs to cooled milk mixture and whisk; add rum or Pisco. Pour mixture over bread. Bake for 30 to 45 minutes, or until the custard is set but still a little wobbly, and edges of bread have browned. Serve warm with white chocolate sauce if desired.

DIRECTIONS FOR WHITE CHOCOLATE SAUCE

1. In a small heavy saucepan, heat the heavy cream until very warm; do not allow it to boil.

2. Add the white chocolate and stir until melted and the mixture is creamy. Don't boil or white chocolate will separate.

*Huesillos (dried peaches) give Pisco a floral scent and unusual flavor,

GUAVANNOLIS

This dessert puts a Peruvian spin on the traditional Italian cannoli.

SERVES 3, OR 6 IF CANNOLI SHELLS ARE HALVED

INGREDIENTS

- » ¼ cup guava paste
- » ¼ cup guava concentrate
- » 1 cup ricotta cheese
- » 2 tablespoons Strega liqueur
- » 3 cannoli shells
- » Pistachio brittle
- » Powdered sugar

CHAPTER 8

SOUTHERN ITALY: A LOVE STORY

Mozzarella – and meeting my wife Anna -- made me fall in love with Southern Italy. It was 4:30 a.m., and I was visiting my future wife's ancestral home in Siano, outside Salerno, for the first time. In the dark outside the second-story bedroom where I was sleeping, there was a cry of "mozzarella, mozzarella." Still groggy from travel, I woke up and peered out into the darkness. Below the window was a motorbike with a cooler attached to the back. A man looked up and motioned to me to come down. "Vieni, Vieni! (Come, Come!)"

PIZZA E MALONE

My wife's aunt, Maria, lives in Siano, in an apartment building filled with family members. A widow who raised her three children on her own, she is a talented and natural cook. On a trip to Southern Italy, she made me a typical Sianese dish, Pizza e Malone. This is not what we think of as pizza, but a thick cornmeal cake, similar to polenta, which is toasted and served with wild local greens -- mallone -- and beans and potatoes. When asked about the origin of the dish, everyone in Siano gave me different versions. Finally, chef and native Mario Nocera explained that peasants of Siano foraged many wild edible greens to make this dish. Nowadays broccoli rabe, dandelion, and sometimes arugula are used. But many Sianese, like Zia Maria, still forage for this dish.

SERVES 4-6 AS AN APPETIZER

INGREDIENTS

Polenta Cake

» 1 quart water
» 1 teaspoon salt

» 1 cup coarse cornmeal
» 1- 2 tablespoons neutral oil, such as canola

DIRECTIONS

1. Bring the water to boil in a large saucepan. Pour in salt and stir to create a well in the center. Slowly pour in cornmeal, stirring constantly. Make sure water continues to boil.

2. When all the cornmeal is added, continue to stir, pulling up mixture from bottom and sides as you stir. Continue to stir until mixture pulls away cleanly from sides, about 35-40 minutes.

3. Allow to cool slightly as you prepare a round pie pan, 10-11 inches in diameter, by lining with plastic wrap or wax paper, covering bottom and sides. Pour polenta into the pan and refrigerate for several hours or overnight.

4. Remove polenta from the refrigerator an hour before toasting. Heat either a large saute pan or a flat-topped griddle, and very lightly skim with neutral oil, such as canola. Slide the polenta cake out of the pie pan and toast on one side. Carefully turn with spatulas to toast the other side. Keep warm.

——— GREENS AND VEGETABLES ———

INGREDIENTS

» ½ pound white beans, such as cannellini, soaked overnight, or 15-ounce canned beans
» 2 quarts greens, mixed broccoli rabe (stems removed), dandelion greens, arugula
» 2 pounds potatoes
» 2 tablespoons extra virgin olive oil

» 2 cloves garlic, sliced thin
» 1 small hot pepper, sliced thin, or 1-2 teaspoons Calabrian chili flakes
» 1 teaspoon dried oregano
» Salt and pepper to taste

129

DIRECTIONS

1. Cover beans with water and bring to boil. Reduce heat to simmer and cook beans until tender, about an hour, depending on the freshness of the beans. Drain, lightly salt, and set aside. Skip this step if using canned beans, simply drain and lightly salt.

2. Bring a large pot of water to boil and add the greens. Boil for 8-10 minutes. Drain and set greens aside to cool in a large bowl.

3. Meanwhile, peel and cut potatoes into eighths. Boil in salted water for 10-12 minutes until tender. Cool slightly, then roughly mash with a fork

4. Using scissors, cut the greens in the bowl in thin strands.

5. Heat olive oil in a saute pan; add garlic and gently saute until tender. Add sliced hot pepper or pepper flakes.

6. Generously salt the greens in the bowl and then add to the oil and garlic. Sprinkle oregano and black pepper over the greens and saute lightly, turning so that greens are seasoned with the garlic and peppers.

TO SERVE

Place polenta cake on a large platter that can be brought to the table. On another platter, mound the greens and then top with the mashed potatoes and beans. Serve by cutting each diner a wedge of toasted polenta and then topping that with greens, potatoes, and beans.

NEW ENGLAND MUSSELS GRATINADOS

Where New England meets Peru and Italy, *in ingredients*

SERVES 2

INGREDIENTS

- » 1 tablespoon extra virgin olive oil
- » 1 garlic clove, minced
- » 16 fresh Maine mussels
- » ½ cup white wine
- » 2 medium potatoes, boiled in salted water for 8-10 minutes until just tender
- » 2 teaspoons bottarga di muggine
- » 1 tablespoon parsley, minced
- » 2 sprigs fresh oregano

DIRECTIONS

1. Heat olive oil in a medium saute pan with a cover, and then add garlic, reducing heat to medium low. Saute until garlic is golden, about 3 minutes. Add mussels and mix. Then add wine and cover the pan until mussels open, about 8 minutes.

2. Using a small ceramic baking pan, remove one side of the shells and place the shell with the flesh on the pan. Using a shredder or microplane, shred boiled potato on top of each mussel, then shred bottarga on top.

3. Place under broiler until shredded potato is crispy, about 3 minutes. Garnish with chopped parsley and oregano.

PACCHERI
WITH MASCARPONE AND SHRIMP

In 2008, I traveled to Italy with my wife, Anna, and stayed in Sorrento for a couple of days. At a small restaurant that had a beautiful view of the sea, one of the dishes was a paccheri pasta. I had never heard of that pasta shape, and I was intrigued by the dish's combination of shrimp, mascarpone, and porcini because I was under the impression that you should never mix land with sea. But on reflection, it started to make sense that there are a lot of ways to combine mushrooms and seafood. In this particular dish, the flavors of porcini, mascarpone, and shrimp complemented each other perfectly. Since that visit, I have made many dishes with paccheri, and often combined shellfish and mushrooms. This quick dish recreates that Sorrento visit with its mingling of the sea and the land.

SERVES 4

INGREDIENTS

» 17 ounces dried paccheri pasta
» 1 ½ tablespoons extra virgin olive oil
» 8 ounces cubed frozen porcini
» 1 garlic clove, chopped fine
» 1 pound white U13 shrimp (13 shrimp to a pound), peeled and deveined
» 2 tablespoons chopped parsley, divided
» Salt, black pepper to taste
» 8 ounces mascarpone, softened
» 2 ounces unsalted butter

DIRECTIONS

1. Defrost the porcini; do not soak or rinse with water. Alternatively, soak the dried porcini in hot water to cover for 10 minutes, drain, saving the water, and chop coarsely.

2. In a large saute pan over medium high heat, heat 1 ½ tablespoons olive oil and add cubed porcini and garlic. Saute 3 minutes until the garlic is golden brown. Add shrimp, stirring; cook for 1 minute. Add half the parsley, salt and pepper to taste, sauteeing until the shrimp begins to turn pink. Lower heat to low, add the mascarpone and butter, stirring slowly to combine, and cook for 5 or 6 more minutes until shrimp is pink and cooked through and the mixture is creamy.

3. Meanwhile, abundantly salt a large pot of water and bring to a boil. Add paccheri and cook at a boil until pasta is al dente; the cooking time for paccheri is about 7-10 minutes.

4. Drain paccheri and mix the pasta into the sauce in the sauce pan. Cook over very low heat for 2 minutes more to give the sauce time to permeate the pasta. Taste for salt and pepper and divide into 4 pasta bowls. Sprinkle each with the remaining tablespoon of chopped parsley

INSALATA DI Baccala

This is a great antipasto dish and very popular in the area of Naples. I learned how to make this from Chef Mario Nocera, who treasures the history of Southern Italian cuisine and ingredients. Natives of Naples and South Italy have traditionally eaten dried cod or "Baccala," heavily salted to preserve it and shipped from Scandinavian countries, to supplement local fish and other proteins. Baccala is often part of the Christmas Eve Feast of the Seven Fishes where Italian extended families gather to enjoy a meatless meal before Christmas Day. Dried cod, sold in slabs in specialty stores, takes time to prepare because it must be soaked and rinsed before using. (See instructions below).

135

SERVES 4 AS FIRST COURSE; 8 AS ANTIPASTO

INGREDIENTS

» 2 pounds Baccala, soaked to desalt *
» 25 black olives
» 25 green olives
» 1 cup mixed diced celery, red bell peppers and carrots
» Salt, black pepper to taste

» 2 tablespoons parsley, chopped fine
» ¼ cup extra virgin olive oil, plus more if desired
» 2 tablespoons white vinegar
» Lemon zest from ½ lemon

DIRECTIONS

1. Cut the desalted cod into small pieces, about 2 inches by 2 inches, and then cook in boiling water for 4 minutes; remove and let cool.

2. When cod is room temperature, in a large bowl, mix cod, olives, diced vegetables and ¼ cup extra virgin olive oil. Add vinegar and lemon zest Season to taste, being careful not to oversalt if cod is still a little salty. Toss all the contents, and add more olive oil if you wish.

3. Chill in the refrigerator for about one hour. Toss again before serving.

Soak cod in cold water to cover in a cool spot or refrigerator for at least 24 hours or up to 3 days, changing the water frequently. Taste to test saltiness; continue soaking if too salty.

BUCATINI
WITH COLATURA DI ALICI

(Adapted from Patricia Malanga of Le Vigne Dei Raito)

This is a typical dish from the Amalfi coast, as made by the winemaker Patricia Malanga at Le Vigne Dei Raito, for her guests. For centuries Colatura di Alici has been produced there, a garum (or juice) of tiny anchovies pressed by hand in a days' long process. This heady elixir is being recognized as a delicacy by many chefs around the world.

SERVES 4-6

INGREDIENTS

» 1 pound of dried bucatini
» 2 garlic cloves, peeled and smashed with a knife
» ½ cup extra virgin olive oil
» 2 or more tablespoons parsley, chopped
» Zest of 1 lemon
» 4 tablespoons of Colatura di Alici
» 1 small hot chili pepper, whole

DIRECTIONS

1. In a medium saute pan, heat the oil and lightly saute smashed garlic cloves for about 2 minutes. Break the chili pepper into three pieces and add to oil. Remove from the stove and add 2 tablespoons of colatura. Pour into a heat-proof mixing bowl; set aside.

2. In a 6-quart pot, boil unsalted water (the colatura will be salty); add pasta and cook until al dente, saving ¼ cup pasta water in a small bowl. Drain pasta and place into a bowl containing the olive oil. Add pasta water little by little if the mixture is dry. Toss and then add the remaining 2 tablespoons of Colatura, and more olive oil if needed. Garnish with chopped parsley and lemon zest. Serve immediately. Once pasta is al dente remove and place in a mixing bowl containing the olive oil mix from the sautee pan, add some pasta water if needed, toss and add the remaining 2 tablespoons of colatura, a bit more of EVOO if needed, garnish with chopped parsley and the zest of ½ lemon.

REGINELLE PIZZAIOLA

Reginelle, candele lunghe, or any large pasta like rigatoni or penne will work here. When a chef uses long cuts such as reginele or candele lunghe, one charming Italian tradition is to have each guest break his or her own pasta into pieces to be added to the pasta pot.

SERVES 4

INGREDIENTS

» 3 tablespoons olive oil
» 3 garlic cloves, chopped
» 1 pound ribeye steak, sliced into pieces about 2 inches long, 1 inch thick
» 1 14.2-ounce can Italian cherry tomatoes

» ¼ cup red wine
» 2 teaspoons dry oregano
» Salt, pepper to taste
» 16- to 17-ounces pasta, large shape such as reginelle or candele
» 1 cup grated Parmesan

DIRECTIONS

1. Heat a saute pan until very hot, add olive oil, garlic and steak. Brown the meat, turning frequently both meat and garlic are golden brown.

2. Using a slotted spoon, remove the steak and garlic to a plate, and deglaze the saute pan with red wine. Add cherry tomatoes and oregano, sauteing for a few minutes. Return the steak and garlic to the pan, sprinkle generously with salt and pepper, and cook over medium-low heat for 30-35 minutes until beef is very tender.

3. Meanwhile, bring a large pot of heavily salted water to a boil. Add the broken pieces of reginelle or candele or other pasta shapes; cook until al dente. Scoop about ½ cup cooking water into a measuring cup. Drain pasta.

4. Toss the pasta with the sauce, adding the reserved pasta cooking water a few tablespoons at a time if the sauce is dry, and cooking over low heat to thicken.

5. Serve with grated Parmesan

BRACIOLA DI CAPRA SIANO (Braciole of Goat)

Braciole, or involtini, are rolls or bundles of thinly sliced meat filled with pecorino cheese, garlic and aromatic herbs, and cooked with tomato sauce. Beef is often used, but this recipe, using goat, has been handed down from generation to generation in the small town of Siano, Italy.

138

Steep pastures and the dry climate are especially suitable for goats. Not surprisingly, thrifty Italian cooks found ways to use the flavorful meat in classic dishes such as this braciole. Although Americans are less familiar with goat meat, it is becoming more readily available in butcher shops and specialty stores. To temper the strong flavor of goat, the rolls are first browned, then braised in white wine before being braised for 2 ½ to 3 hours until the meat is fork tender.

SERVES 4

INGREDIENTS

- » 8 slices of goat meat (from top of leg or shoulder), very thinly sliced (beef flank steak can be substituted)
- » Coarse salt and black pepper
- » ⅔ cup pecorino cheese, grated
- » 1 small onion, finely chopped
- » ½ cup flat-leaf parsley, chopped
- » Butchers twine
- » 2 tablespoons extra-virgin olive oil
- » 1 ½ cups white wine
- » ½ cup white vinegar
- » 5 cloves garlic, peeled and chopped
- » Simple Tomato Sauce (Page XX)

BRACIOLA DI CAPRA SIANO

DIRECTIONS

1. Place the pieces of meat (about 1-inch thick) on a cutting board and season with salt, pepper, 3 chopped garlic cloves, grated pecorino, chopped parsley, leaving an inch of space around edges.

2. Roll them up and tie them with butcher's twine.

3. Heat olive oil in a deep skillet with a cover or a Dutch oven. Add the bundles of meat. Brown on all sides over medium heat, turning carefully to not dislodge the filling.

4. Add white wine, vinegar and 2 garlic cloves to the pan, scraping any pan juices from the browning. Raise heat until wine comes to a boil, then immediately reduce heat to medium low and braise for 20 minutes.

5. Add tomato sauce to the skillet or Dutch oven. The sauce should almost cover the meat rolls. Add a little water if there isn't enough sauce to cover.

6. Braise for 2 ½ to 3 hours over medium low to low heat, checking now and then to make sure there is enough liquid to almost cover the rolls.

7. Remove from heat, cut and remove the string. Serve with pasta of your choice, spooning the meaty tomato sauce over the pasta.

CHOCOLATE EGGPLANT
WITH PERUVIAN SAN RAMON CACAO

When we opened Taranta we wanted to be as Southern Italian as possible. My partner at the time, Mario Nocera, recalled a very unusual dessert from Campania that had originated in a Franciscan monastery. It appears from time to time on our menu, and is easily made at home.

140 **SERVES 6-8**

INGREDIENTS

- » 2 pounds eggplant, preferably Japanese variety
- » 4 teaspoons salt
- » 6 large eggs, lightly beaten
- » 2 cups unseasoned bread crumbs
- » 2 cups canola oil
- » 2 ounces unsweetened condensed milk
- » ½ cup sugar
- » 6 tablespoons unsweetened cocoa powder
- » 2 teaspoons cornstarch
- » 1 ounce dark Peruvian 70 % chocolate
- » 1 tablespoon unsalted butter
- » 2 ounces aromatic liqueur, such as Cointreau or orange-infused Pisco
- » 1 cup candied orange peel or mixed candied fruit
- » ⅓ cup pine nuts

CHOCOLATE EGGPLANT

DIRECTIONS

1. Peel the eggplant and slice it into thin pieces. In a shallow dish or pan, layer the eggplant, salting each layer as you go. Next, place a plate on top of the eggplant layers and add some weight, such as a large can of tomatoes or a couple of bricks, to apply pressure. Allow this to sit for approximately 2 hours. This will help the eggplant release excess moisture.

2. After 2 hours, rinse the eggplant slices to remove the salt, and then pat them dry using clean dish towels. Put back into the dish and cover with beaten eggs. Allow to soak to absorb egg mixture for a few minutes.

3. Spread bread crumbs evenly on a large plate or platter. Dip each eggplant slice in the breadcrumbs to coat them. In a deep-sided sauté pan, heat the oil until it shimmers. Fry the eggplant slices on each side until they turn a golden brown color; do this in batches, don't crowd or overlay the slices. Once fried, place them on paper towels to drain and cool.

4. To make the chocolate sauce, combine condensed milk, sugar, cocoa powder, cornstarch, and 1 cup of cold water in a medium saucepan. Whisk thoroughly until all the ingredients are well blended. Heat this mixture over medium-high heat until it comes to a boil, then reduce the heat to medium. Stir constantly and allow it to simmer until the sauce thickens, which should take about 3 minutes. Let the mixture cool for a few minutes, then stir in the butter and chocolate until they melt. Optionally, add Cointreau or Pisco for flavor.

5. As though assembling a lasagna, layer the fried eggplant slices and chocolate sauce on a serving platter or in a shallow baking pan. Finish by topping it with the remaining chocolate sauce, and garnish with candied fruit and pine nuts. Serve cold.

ZIA MARIA MAKES PIZZA E MALLONE

Maria diFilippo welcomes us into her apartment in Siano, Italy. Her extended family lives in this building -- a sister-in-law and her husband, and two sons and their families -- children and adults tumbling in and out of each others' homes.

Maria, tiny and perpetually smiling, is going to show us how to make pizza e mallone, an old Campania dish that illustrates how Southern Italians turn humble and often wild ingredients into delicious and nourishing dishes. On holiday from her job cooking at a school, she has been working all morning. One of the "pizzas," not what we think of as pizza but a white corn polenta cake, crumbled as she flipped it to brown the other side, but she succeeds with the second, expertly nudging it over so that both sides are a toasty brown. "The important thing is that we have one that turns out good," she says as the photographer leans in for a shot.

On the back of the small stove, potatoes are boiling, and on the table is a container of broccoli rabe that she asks us to stem. Although in summer the dish would include a "mallone" of seven or eight varieties of wild greens, only a few leafy vegetables can be found now in the hills above town. Maria has also braised cannellini beans, which she purchased fresh from the market.

Her kitchen is a marvel of compact efficiency. As she works, she carries dishes to the terrace to cool, and runs to the back terrace behind her bedroom to pick a few hot peppers. Behind a door hang sausages to keep them from her sons, who sometimes roam through looking for a snack. What was once a fireplace is covered by a seat cushion to hide dry goods, and the small refrigerator is in the sitting room area.

She stops cooking for a few minutes to offer espresso to her guests, making a perfect brew in a 35-year-old stovetop coffee pot. Her daughter bought her a new one, she explains, but it didn't make good coffee so she threw it out.

She puts the greens into a big pot of boiling water, and peels and chops garlic. That goes into a small skillet coated with olive oil along with a few chopped hot peppers. The cooked greens are cut with scissors and then are added to the oil and garlic,

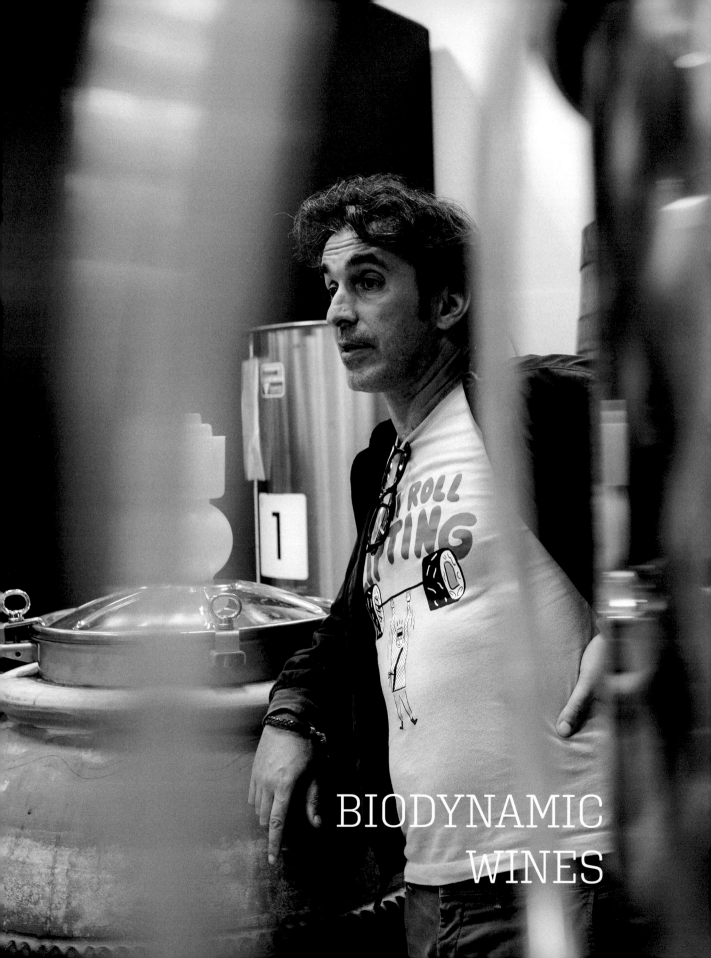

BIODYNAMIC
WINES

At Taranta, we served only biodynamic wines, part of my quest for sustainability, and continue to offer some at Tambo. Although sometimes sourcing these wines from small producers can be difficult and my wine menus did not carry some of the most profitable big-name vintages, the decision was not only an ecological one, but also defined Taranta's goals. And we still feel the wine is much better and healthier for our customers.

I was introduced to biodynamic wines by Marco Marrocco, who produces all natural Palazzo Tronconi wines in Lazio, south of Rome. Along with others, he had rejected the conventional wisdom in modern winemaking and returned to a pact with nature. Following the teachings of Rudolph Steiner, an Austrian who championed fertilizing with a cow horn filled with fermented dung and other naturalistic methods, Marrocco composts the earth around his vines with grasses and grains, fertilizes naturally, and keeps honey bees, using the propyls they produce in their hives to protect the vines. These traditions forgo chemicals to produce wine that is alive and tastes of its terroir.

Others such as the Salerno family at Casa di Baal near Salerno use similar methods. In fact, Anibale Salerno, who has been farming olive trees, vegetables and vineyards organically for decades, insists these methods are more cost-effective because it requires no purchases of synthetic chemicals. To him and other biodynamic wine makers, following these ways honors the agriculture of long ago when the farmer listened to the earth. The Casa di Baal farm stresses using local grape and olive varieties, and embraces diversity in the vineyards that are filled with bees, birds and native plants.

At Le Vigne di Raito near Salerno, winemaker Patrizia Malanga tends a very small and very vertical vineyard that produces stellar vintages using the same principles as those at Casa di Baal and Tronconi. A chic and very modern woman, she still swears by the efficacy of burying a cow horn filled with manure in her vineyards and giving bees and natural plants room amid her vines.

We started serving biodynamic wines when the practice was unusual. These wines are alive. You open one bottle, taste and marvel, and then the next might be different. But the spirit of the winemakers, the terroir of the land, and the natural flavors make them vibrant and exciting to us and to our customers.

Bobby Eustace, Owner
of Polcari's Coffee

One day, I walked into Abruzzo's Meat Market on Salem Street, and met Joe and Frank Susi. I was trying to figure out whether to open a restaurant or work in hotels, and was feeling unsettled and a little out of place. The Susis were welcoming and supportive, and invited me to spend time there. In the back they'd make lunch – wild mushrooms with pasta, a glass of homemade wine, espresso made in a stovetop machine. They'd talk about Italy and about food, and Joe, who had lived in Venezuela for a time, happily included a South American into the conversations. It was apparent that their human values could knit together two very different cultures. Their families and others in the community kept up the traditions of Italy, and the North End felt more like Europe. It even smelled like Europe, the way the neighborhood looked, the way the ladies hung their laundry out the windows, and, of course, the food.

150

The North End has a long history as the first stop for immigrants, from Irish to Jews to African Americans to Jewish immigrants. But the Italian wave that began in the early 1900s, driven by poverty in their native country, was imprinted on the neighborhood and became its lasting character. Living crowded into the cold water tenements that had been built for Irish workers, the new arrivals worked in factories, as laborers and masons, as fishermen, and their restaurants, cafes, churches and schools marked the North End as Little Italy.

The neighborhood has changed a lot over the years. The history – Paul Revere's house, the Freedom Trail, the Old North Church – is still there, but there are fewer and fewer Italians living in the area. Tourists still flock here for all the restaurants, but the old stores are mostly gone. Traditions are being lost; in fact, now that her mother is gone, my wife can't find anyone to talk with in her Southern Italian dialect.

But sometimes on a Sunday morning, you can catch the old timers hanging out at a cafe or during festival time in August see tourists mingling with Italian families that may no longer live in the North End but come back to remember where their parents and grandparents lived when they arrived. In the North End, so many newcomers have found a safe place in the New World.

CHAPTER 9

HUARIPAMPA: LAND OF TOMORROW

S ustainability comes in many forms. To many, sustaining the earth and the environment are its crucial elements. To me, there's another, perhaps more important, one -- social impact, the human element. The social impact of what I do on my family, my staff, my communities has been enlarged and invigorated by the inhabitants of a village called Huaripampa in the Central Highlands of Peru.

Visitors to Peru tend to hop from Lima to the ruins of Machu Picchu with a stopover in Cusco in the Sacred Valley. Although the enduring fascination of Machu Picchu demands a visit, it has been so overrun with tourists that limits have been instituted. But these days, trekkers and more adventurous tourists are beginning to head north of Lima to a land of breathtaking peaks and valleys less known, but even more spectacular in natural beauty than the ancient Incan capital. La Cordillera Blanca is the highest range outside the Himalayas, and Europeans especially flock to scale almost 20,000-foot Artesonraju or the Paramount (from which Paramount Pictures logo may have been derived) and trek the steep paths to jewels such as the glacier-fed Lake Paron, as blue as the Caribbean Sea although its altitude is more than 13,000 feet.

In a valley near the entrance to the Santa Cruz trek path sits the village of Huaripampa, home to a few hundred people, with a school, a small tienda (store), and roaming chickens and pigs. Nearby is my family's Santa Cruz Lodge, which we have been developing as a retreat for trekkers and seekers of peace and beauty. Though the lodge is a commercial venture, the aim is broader: Its activity

Recipes:
- » Roxana's LLunca Soup
- » Jose's Smoked Fava Beans
- » Quinoa Carretilera (Breakfast Drink)
- » Pachamanca a la Olla

155

is dedicated to improving the lives
of those in Huaripampa. Not only do
villagers work building and maintaining
the lodge, but young men and women
are trained in culinary skills. Funds
from the lodge and visitors' donations
provide equipment, furniture and
supplies for the local school. Skilled
guides lead visitors on the winding
trails and steep hikes in the mountain
passes.

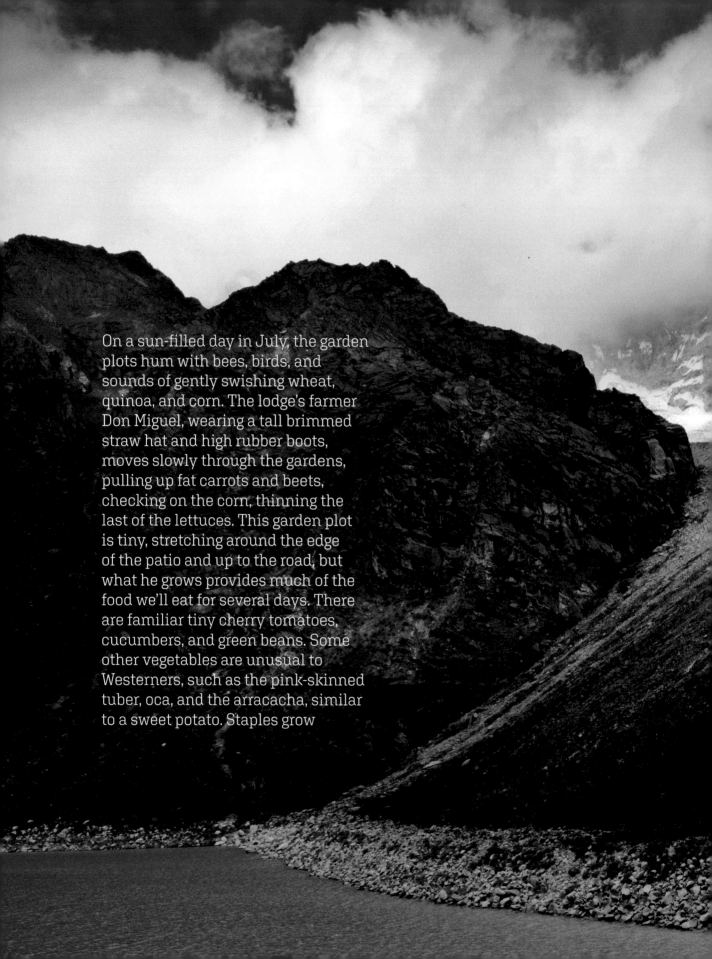

On a sun-filled day in July, the garden plots hum with bees, birds, and sounds of gently swishing wheat, quinoa, and corn. The lodge's farmer Don Miguel, wearing a tall brimmed straw hat and high rubber boots, moves slowly through the gardens, pulling up fat carrots and beets, checking on the corn, thinning the last of the lettuces. This garden plot is tiny, stretching around the edge of the patio and up to the road, but what he grows provides much of the food we'll eat for several days. There are familiar tiny cherry tomatoes, cucumbers, and green beans. Some other vegetables are unusual to Westerners, such as the pink-skinned tuber, oca, and the arracacha, similar to a sweet potato. Staples grow

abundantly, with several crops
a year of quinoa, dried beans,
potatoes, and large-kerneled corn.
The grains, beans and corn provide
ingredients for soups and porridge-
like breakfast drinks, the hearty
food that sustains natives and
tourists in the thin, cold air.

ROXANA'S LLUNCA SOUP

Soups are ubiquitous in the highlands of Peru, a way to fortify laborers in the fields or towns or sustain trekkers in the thin Andean atmosphere. Roxana, who works for me at the Santa Cruz Lodge, calls this soup "slippery" because of the trigo, or wheat, it contains. Her version includes wheat, beans, vegetables, and herbs from the lodge gardens and chicken raised locally. Although in Peru, a variety of wheat called shambar might be used, in North America wheat berries or even farro can be substituted. This soup takes a long time to cook, but isn't difficult to make, and is good the next day.

SERVES 6

INGREDIENTS

- » 1 ¼ cups durum wheat berries, soaked overnight, or farro (no soaking needed)
- » 1 ½ cups white beans, such as cannellini, soaked overnight
- » 2 teaspoons salt, divided
- » 8 cups or more water
- » 1 3-4 pound chicken cut into pieces
- » 1 tablespoon thyme leaves, chopped
- » 1 tablespoon parsley, chopped
- » 2 yellow potatoes, scrubbed and cubed
- » 2 carrots, peeled and sliced
- » 1 ½ tablespoons olive oil
- » 2 cloves garlic, chopped
- » 1 large onion, chopped
- » 1 aji amarillo, chopped fine, or 2 teaspoons amarillo paste
- » 1 Colorado chili, or 2 serrano chilies, chopped fine
- » 1 teaspoon cumin
- » 1 bunch cilantro, chopped

ROXANA'S LLUNCA SOUP

DIRECTIONS

1. Put the soaked wheat berries, farro and soaked beans in a large soup pot; add enough cold water to cover by 2 inches, and add 1 teaspoon salt. Bring to boil; reduce heat to a simmer; add more water if necessary. Cook for 25 minutes.

2. Add chicken pieces, 1 teaspoon salt and enough water to cover the chicken. Bring to boil, reduce heat to simmer, and skim any foam from the surface. Cook for 20 minutes, and then add potatoes and carrots. Cook for another 25 minutes until vegetables, beans, and chicken are tender and cooked through.

3. In a separate skillet, heat the olive oil and add the onion and garlic. Saute 7 minutes until the onion is soft. Add the peppers or paste, cumin, ½ teaspoon salt, 1 teaspoon pepper and saute until peppers are soft and fragrant. Add to the soup pot with half the cilantro. Cook for another 30 minutes.

4. Serve in deep soup bowls, sprinkling more cilantro on top. Choclo (large-kerneled corn on cob) can be served on the side.

165

FAVAS WITH SMOKED SALT

These fava beans are the Peruvian answer to edamame, an addictive little snack to serve with your favorite Pisco cocktail, wine or beer. Healthy, quick to make, and with a sophisticated twist, you'll find yourself adding them to any cocktail party or appetizer menu.

166

SERVES 4-6 AS APPETIZER

INGREDIENTS

- » 2 pounds fresh fava beans, in shells
- » 1 tablespoon olive oil
- » 1 tablespoon Himalayan or other smoked salt
- » ½ cup water

DIRECTIONS

1. Heat a large cast iron skillet on top of the stove or over wood or charcoal fire. Add olive oil and heat.

2. Throw in fava beans and sprinkle with smoked salt. Using two spoons or sturdy tongs, turn the favas several times, allowing the shells to blacken in spots. This should take about 10 minutes.

4. Turn again and then add water. Cover pan and allow favas to steam for 5 minutes.

5. Remove from the skillet with tongs or spoons, shaking gently to remove any water clinging to the shells. Serve on a large platter or in a basket. Guests and diners will peel the favas themselves. These are good served with a slightly salty pecorino or goat cheese.

QUINOA CARRETILERA

This is a hot breakfast drink designed to give farm workers in the high altitude of the Andes plenty of energy for their tasks. It's simple to make, with or without the addition of chuño, the freeze-dried potato used to thicken liquids.

SERVES 4

INGREDIENTS

- » 1 cup white quinoa
- » 1 large apple, peeled and chopped
- » ½ pineapple, peeled and cut into chunks
- » 2 cups water
- » 1 teaspoon cinnamon
- » 3 cloves
- » 2 tablespoons chuño (optional) or 2 tablespoons pineapple gelatin
- » 1 tablespoon honey or to taste

DIRECTIONS

1. Combine quinoa, fruit, water, cinnamon and cloves in a saucepan. Bring to boil over medium heat, reduce to a simmer. Cook for 20 minutes until quinoa has sprouted and is tender.

2. Slowly add chuño or gelatin, stirring to combine. Let simmer for a few minutes more. Remove cloves. Add honey or sugar to taste. Serve in mugs to drink.

PACHAMANCA A LA OLLA

This ancient Incan recipe is traditionally cooked outside under a covering of earth and stones. In the highlands of Peru, a variety of meats -- alpaca, cuy (guinea pig), lamb and vicuña -- might be included. Here, the ingredient list is simplified, and corn husks help create the moist heat to replicate the earthen oven. Nevertheless, this Pachamanca is a delicious invocation of an ancient tradition.

SERVES 8

INGREDIENTS

» 2 pounds pork belly, cut into 6-ounce pieces
» 4 chicken thighs
» 4 chicken drumsticks
» Salt and pepper to taste
» 2 teaspoons cumin or more to taste
» 2 tablespoons Peruvian garlic paste
» 2 tablespoons panca pepper paste
» 3 tablespoons mild aji amarillo paste
» ½ cup huacatay (Peruvian black mint)
» 3 tablespoons chopped cilantro
» 3 tablespoons vegetable oil
» 1 cup of Chicha de Jora (fermented Peruvian corn cider)
» 2 pounds fresh fava beans, in a shell
» 2 pounds small sweet potatoes
» 2 pounds small yellow potatoes
» 4 giant Peruvian corn on cob (sold frozen in specialty stores)
» 1 cup water
» 2 tablespoons white vinegar
» Corn husks (available at some groceries or specialty stores)

DIRECTIONS

1. In a very large bowl or roasting pan, season all the meats with salt, pepper, and cumin to your taste. Add garlic, panca, and aji amarillo pastes, and stir to ensure the meat is coated evenly.

2. In a blender, combine huacatay, cilantro, 3 tablespoons of vegetable oil, half a teaspoon of salt, and 2 tablespoons of water. Blend until you have a paste-like consistency. Stir this mixture into the seasoned meats.

3. Combine potatoes, sweet potatoes, fava beans, and Chicha de Jora corn with the meat and spice mixture. Mix everything thoroughly, then refrigerate for approximately 3 hours to allow the flavors to marinate.

4. In a large braising pot, ideally clay or terracotta, create a layer of corn husks at the bottom. Place the pork belly, followed by the chicken on top. Layer the potatoes, corn, and fava beans over the meat. Spread the remaining marinade on top. Add a cup of water and 2 tablespoons of vinegar.

5. Cover the top with corn husks and then place the lid on the pot.

6. Cook over medium heat for about 1 ½ hours.

7. Serve on a tray, including all the flavorful juices.

BASIC RECIPES

SALSA CRIOLLA • SIMPLE TOMATO SAUCE • AJI AMARILLO AIOLI

SALSA CRIOLLA

A favorite among Peruvians is the "Salsita Criolla" a traditional topping that is served very often with Peruvian Dishes or just by itself.

INGREDIENTS

- » 2 medium-sized red onions
- » Juice of 2 limes
- » 1 tablespoon parsley
- » 2 tablespoons vegetable oil or extra virgin olive oil
- » Salt and pepper to taste
- » 1 tablespoon diced aji amarillo

DIRECTIONS

1. Peel onions and slice very thinly, then rinse and soak in cold water with a few ice cubes added.
2. Strain water from onions.
3. In a small metal bowl, mix all the ingredients, toss, add salt and pepper, toss again and serve. Keep refrigerated until serving..

SIMPLE TOMATO SAUCE

INGREDIENTS

- » 2 tablespoons olive oil
- » 1 medium onion, diced
- » 1 clove garlic, chopped fine
- » 1 24-ounce can crushed or diced whole good-quality tomatoes
- » ¼ cup Italian parsley, chopped
- » Salt and pepper to taste

172

DIRECTIONS

1. Heat a saute pan or deep saucepan and add olive oil.

2. Add chopped onion and saute over medium heat for 8 minutes until onion is softened. Add garlic and saute 2 minutes, making sure it doesn't burn.

3. Add tomatoes and stir. Bring to a boil and then reduce heat to medium low. Add parsley and salt and pepper. Let sauce simmer for 20 minutes, adding a few tablespoons of water if it seems too dry.

AJI AMARILLO AIOLI

INGREDIENTS

- » 3 eggs
- » 1 ½ cups olive oil
- » 2 teaspoons lime or lemon juice
- » 1 teaspoon aji amarillo paste

DIRECTIONS

173

1. Using an immersion blender, put eggs in a large bowl, and blend for a few seconds to mix. Begin adding olive oil drop by drop, blending constantly until mixture is thick and emulsified.

2. Slowly add the lemon or lime juice, and then blend in the aji amarillo paste. Taste to see if more paste is desired.

SOURCES AND
GLOSSARY

Aji Amarillo paste

Paste from Peruvian yellow chile; the pepper turns red as it matures; hot but balanced with a bit of fruitiness; the paste is available at Peruvian and Latin American markets and online.

Aji Panca paste

Paste from panca chile, dark red and milder than the aji Amarillo; paste is available at Peruvian and Latin American markets and online.

Bacalao, Baccala

Dried salted codfish -- bacalao in Spanish or Portuguese; baccala in Italian -- is a centuries-old way to preserve fish; used in many cultures; must be reconstituted by soaking in water and rinsing repeatedly. Can be found in some groceries and Italian food shops.

Bottarga di Muggine

The salted, pressed and dried roe sack of cod, it is also known as "the poor man's caviar." Usually shaved or finely sliced, it has a salty, slightly nutty umami. Can be found in Italian food shops and online.

Bojita olives

These dark, almost black olives which are meaty and full-flavored are an heirloom variety first cultivated in Peru in the 16th century by the Spanish. Available at Latin American food markets and online.

Cancha corn

A large-kernel corn that has been soaked in water to puff and then fried with salt until crunchy. Used as a snack or topping. Available premade at Latin American markets and online.

Cape Gooseberries

Also called golden berries or Peruvian ground cherries. From the nightshade family (tomatoes, eggplant, tomatillos), they are both sweet and tart, and work well in both sweet and savory dishes. Available at specialty stores and supermarkets.

Chica de Jora

Also called corn beer, this is a fermented beverage made from maize. If purple corn is used it is called Chica de Morada. It sometimes contains a small amount of alcohol. Available at Latin American markets and online.

Chifa

Chinese immigrants to Peru at the beginning of the 19th century brought their cuisine with them, and Peruvians adapted it to native ingredients. The culinary tradition continues today and there are many Peruvian-Chinese fusion dishes. Chef Duarte's family gathers on Sunday evenings for chifa.

Chirimoya

Also called custard apple, this unusual semi-tropical fruit has a scaly skin and, when ripe, a soft, custardy interior. The flavor ranges from mildly sweet to slightly tangy, and is Chef Duarte's favorite fruit. Available in specialty grocers or Latin supermarkets.

Chuño

Potatoes that are freeze-dried in an ancient Andean method of submerging them in very cold, running water and then drying them in bright sunlight. The dehydration process preserves them, and they can be reconstituted and are often used to thicken sauces. Available in Latin American markets and online.

Colatura di Alici

Translated as "anchovy drippings," this clear, very strongly flavored liquid is pressed from anchovies in a long, slow method. Only a little is needed to flavor pastas. Available in Italian specialty stores and online.

Garlic paste

Peruvian garlic paste, ajo molido in Spanish, is a little more concentrated than chopped garlic. Available in Peruvian and Latin American markets and online.

Huacatay

Also called Peruvian black mint, this herb from the marigold family is aromatic and strongly flavored, and is widely used in Peruvian cuisine. Available frozen at Peruvian and Latin American markets.

Lucuma

A favorite fruit of Peru and other Andean countries, lucuma is also called "egg fruit" because of its oval shape. With its delicate flavor and slight sweetness, it's usually used in desserts such as ice cream but sometimes also in savory dishes. Though rarely found fresh, powdered lucuma is available in Peruvian and Latin American markets.

Lupini beans

Called tarwi in Peruvian cuisine, these beans from the pea family are very high in protein. If raw, the beans must be soaked and rinsed repeatedly to remove toxins. Canned or jarred lupini have been treated to be safe for consumption. Available in groceries and specialty stores.

Pallares

Also called giant Peruvian lima beans, pallares are large and white with a creamy, meaty texture. Available in Peruvian and Latin American markets and online.

Papa Seca

Spanish for dried potatoes, these are first boiled and then dried in the hot sun to preserve them. Available in Peruvian and Latin American markets and online.

Rocoto pepper paste

Rocoto peppers are dark red and very spicy, much hotter than jalapenos. The paste is available in Peruvian markets and online.

Sources

Many US cities, such as Boston, New York, and Miami, have small stores that carry Peruvian as well as other Latin American products.

AUTHOR BIOS

Jose Duarte is a chef, a restaurateur, a teacher, an advocate of Peru and its many delicious foods and fascinating culture. But he is also a visionary about what food, health and the environment means for our future and those of our children. A native of Lima, Peru, he was always fascinated by food, cooking, and entertaining. His mother, Ines Duarte, says that as a young boy, he would create entire menus for adult parties, doing all the cooking, arranging the table, and greeting the guests.

Chef Duarte's life followed the arc of a culinary and hospitality career. In 2000, he opened Taranta in the North End of Boston with his wife, Anna. At first designed to be a Southern Italian restaurant, Taranta morphed into a cutting-edge fusion of Peruvian ingredients with the cooking and exuberance of Italy.

Sustainability is at the core of Chef Duarte's philosophy and was the guiding rule of Taranta. Chef Duarte and his staff did composting, used recyclable materials, water-saving methods, and recycled cooking oil. He taught Corporate Team Building classes at the restaurant that had a sustainability emphasis while teaching cooking techniques and developing interpersonal relationships. He has been equally active as a speaker and panel participant on seafood and restaurant sustainability at Massachusetts Institute of Technology, Harvard Extension, New England Aquarium and elsewhere.

The human element of sustainability is another passion. Chef Duarte was a co-producer with author Barry Estabrook and others of the documentary "Fair Tomatoes," in which he appeared. Later he spoke on panels on the issue of human slavery in the tomato industry and Immokalee workers at the Massachusetts Institute of Technology and Bentley University in the Boston area, and Lynn University in Florida and other colleges and universities. In November 2017, he spoke at the United Nations as part of the Latin American Impact Summit on his project to build a lodge at Huaripampa, Peru, that will aid workers and residents while upholding sustainable practices. In 2023, Chef Duarte participated in the film 'Indigenize the Plate' alongside the film's host Natalie Benally. The film, which showcases Chef's work in sustainability and with the lodge and the residents of Huaripampa, was backed by the Corporation for Public Broadcasting and is being distributed by American Public Television for public television and streaming through PBS Passport.

Chef Duarte has appeared on PBS's Neighborhood Kitchens, on Boston Channel 5's Chronicle, PBS radio, numerous times on Boston's TV Diner, and on CNN Espanol, speaking about going green. In early 2015, he was a judge in the finals of Top Chef Estrellas on Telemundo.

 Chef Duarte and his wife Anna also are part owners of two other restaurants, Tambo 22, a Peruvian restaurant in Chelsea, MA, and Trattoria San Pietro, an Italian restaurant in Norwell, MA. They have two children, Sofia and Diego, who love to eat.

Alison Arnett is a journalist and freelance writer specializing in food and agriculture topics. After many years as a newspaper editor, she was for 15 years the Boston Globe's restaurant critic and food writer. Along with thousands of restaurant reviews, she has written about food trends, profiled chefs, cheesemakers, farmers, horticulturalists teaching in Massachusetts prisons, food security, and about the Farm Bill for the Boston Globe Business and Food sections, Edible Boston, Yankee Magazine and elsewhere. A native of a small agricultural village in western Kansas and the oldest of a family of eight children, her ties to agriculture and sustaining a way of life that is disappearing run deep. Mother of two, she hopes that the future holds a sustainable life for her three grandchildren and those who succeed us.

ACKNOWLEDGEMENTS

When I was a teen, I recall jotting down recipes in a school notebook, and remember preparing a meal for my cousins in Venuzuela that was so successful –sweet and sour pork chops – that I knew I had to document it. Although I had always thought about writing a cookbook during my years at Taranta, the idea of creating a book that encapsulated my journey as a chef didn't take shape until I spoke with Alison Arnett, a well-known food writer in Boston. She wholeheartedly embraced my vision of combining recipes and stories. After several years of numerous virtual meetings, phone calls, emails, interviews, and travels to Southern Italy, the Central Andean Region of Peru, and the Amazonia, we finally have a finished product. I want to extend my gratitude to Alison for her patience and unwavering commitment to the project.

As I shaped the concept for this book and considered how readers would engage with it, I had the privilege of meeting the late Peter Miller and his daughter, Liseanne, while they were dining at Taranta. That night, he offered to help find a publisher, and had no doubt that he could bring this book to life. I'm grateful to have crossed paths with him and appreciate his trust in representing an unconventional book concept. In the same spirit, I'd like to thank Charlie Sarabian and Liseanne Miller for carrying forward Peter's legacy and tirelessly working to fulfill his vision.

This book has been influenced by many remarkable people whom I'd like to thank:

My grandfather, Enrique Duarte, who, before his passing, passed down to me his most cherished possession, a Peruvian Chinese recipe book. His stories, extensive knowledge of food and wine, were impressive, and they ignited my curiosity for food.

My grandmother, Paulina Duarte, who continually challenged me to try new flavors, ingredients, and cooking techniques, and who always indulged me with my favorite dishes when I visited her in Peru.

My uncle, Atilio Galindo "Tilin," for inviting a 10-year-old me to dine at exclusive closed-door restaurants in Lima, where the finest food was served.

Chef Javier Wong, who provided my first culinary epiphany when he presented a jumbo summer flounder and asked if we preferred ceviche or tiradito. In a matter of minutes, he transformed the ingredient into a magical dish, a moment that remains vivid to this day.

Chef John Mondone, during my years at Lynn University, for teaching me that cooking without passion is unthinkable, and that perseverance, respect, communication, and organization are crucial elements in a chef's career.

I'd like to express my deep appreciation to my parents, Enrique Duarte and Ines de Duarte, for their sacrifices and unwavering support, providing me with an excellent education and enabling me to pursue my career.

I owe a debt of gratitude to many individuals who played pivotal roles in this project:

My cousin Elke Neustadtl, one of my most ardent supporters throughout my journey as a chef, who is generously sharing her culinary passion and creative talents as a graphic artist, always envisioning the potential of this book and offering invaluable advice.

Daniela Talavera, also a cousin and a talented photographer, who, on short notice, packed her bags and traveled to Italy, Boston, and Huaripampa and the Amazonian region of Peru to capture the striking images featured in the book.

Ricardo Flores, affectionately known as "Tono," who began as a dishwasher on Taranta's very first day and became the last person to leave when we closed the restaurant, essentially overseeing the kitchen. His unwavering loyalty, responsibility, and tireless work ethic are deeply appreciated.

Chef Mario Nocera, the creative force behind the original Taranta Southern Italian concept, for his profound knowledge of traditional cuisine has been a constant source of inspiration and information for this book.

A special thanks goes to my wife, Anna, for her boundless love and support, and to my children, Diego and Sofia, for being the most discerning recipe testers.

INDEX